Guerrilla Selling

Also by Jay Conrad Levinson

The Most Important $1.00 Book Ever Written

Secrets of Successful Free-lancing

San Francisco: An Unusual Guide to Unusual Shopping
(with Pat Levinson and John Bear)

Earning Money Without a Job

555 Ways to Earn Extra Money

150 Secrets of Successful Weight Loss
(with Michael Lavin and Michael Rokeach, M.D.)

Guerrilla Marketing

Guerrilla Marketing Attack

Guerrilla Marketing Weapons

An Earthling's Guide to Satellite TV

Small Business Savvy

Quit Your Job!

The 90-Minute Hour

Guerrilla Financing
(with Bruce Jan Blechman)

GUERRILLA SELLING

Unconventional Weapons and Tactics for Increasing Your Sales

**Bill Gallagher, Ph.D.,
Orvel Ray Wilson, *and* Jay Conrad
Levinson**
Author of *Guerrilla Marketing*

Houghton Mifflin Company
Boston   New York   London   1992

For information about permission to reproduce selections from this book, write to Permissions, Houghton Mifflin Company, 215 Park Avenue South, New York, New York 10003.

Library of Congress Cataloging-in-Publication Data

Gallagher, Bill.
   Guerrilla selling : unconventional weapons and tactics for making the sale / Bill Gallagher, Orvel Ray Wilson, and Jay Conrad Levinson.
      p.   cm.
   Includes bibliographical references and index.
   ISBN 0-395-58039-0
   1. Selling.   I. Wilson, Orvel Ray.   II. Levinson, Jay Conrad.   III. Title.
   HF5438.25.G35   1991   91-34463
   658.8'5—dc20   CIP

Printed in the United States of America

AGM 10 9 8 7 6 5 4 3 2 1

This book is dedicated, first, to our wives—
Dee Dee, Denise, and Pat—and, second, to
the multimillionaires who will earn their next
million as guerrilla salespeople

Contents

Acknowledgments

Guerrilla Selling exists because of the thousands of people who get up every morning and go to work, lubricating the mechanism of free enterprise. From shops and shows and street corners they sell everything from advertising to x-ray machines, all new and improved. They make our high standard of living possible and accelerate the advancement of technology. They're the unsung heroes of American business.

For years, the three of us have led seminars and training workshops on sales, marketing, and management, and we've had the privilege of working with some of the most successful business people in the world. Along the way they've shared their frustrations, their triumphs, and their secrets, and these are the same people who have encouraged us to put it in writing and share it with the world. Our gratitude extends to them all.

Scores of fellow guerrillas have contributed to the ideas we've assembled here. None of it is totally new or completely original, but the stories are real-life, the examples are real-world, and they *really* work.

Specifically, we'd like to thank Dr. William Shear at Guerrilla Marketing International who first envisioned *Guerrilla Selling*, Mike Larsen, our agent, who pushed that vision into book form, and Henry Ferris and Erika Mansourian, our editors, who found it "incredibly inspiring."

"The Mind Map" evolved from the work of our teachers Jean Piaget, Leonard Newmark, Vern Black, Vernon Woolf, Steve and Connirae Andreas, Tom McDonald, Robert Ornstein, and Richard F. Thompson.

NaB and CaPTuRe was developed under the supervision of Jack Riley with input from Boyd Watkins. Earlier versions were developed with suggestions from Gordon Hawkins and Jay Horrocks.

Our fellow authors Tom Peters, John Naisbitt, Dr. Carl Sagan, Alvin Toffler, Harvey Mackay, Larry Wilson, Dr. Tony Alessandra, Frank

Bettger, Dr. Ken Blanchard, Dr. Richard M. Restak, Elmer Wheeler, Phil Wexler, Robert Miller, Maria Arapakis, Brian Tracy, Stephen R. Covey, Dr. Douglas Merrill, Hank Trisler, Tom Hopkins, Joe Girard, Zig Ziglar, and Dr. David Schwartz have influenced our point of view through their written contributions to the field of professional sales.

Jim Cathcart, Patricia Fripp, Jeff Slutsky, Geof Cook, Mike Lavin, Wyatt Riberich, Deirdre Gallagher, Denise Wilson, and Lou Pinder have contributed personal stories and examples.

We are particularly indebted to Dr. Alan N. Schoonmaker, Paul Myers, J. Douglas Edwards, David Sandler, James S. Scherrer, Dick Atwood, Brian Azar, Gerhard Gschwandtner, Tony Lore, Dottie Walters, and Bruce Jan Blechman for personally contributing material, ideas, philosophies, and suggestions, all of which we liberally incorporated.

Patrick R. McConnell, Robert Gallagher, Robert N. Brown, Dr. Sanford Danziger, Harold Johnson, William Gallagher, Jr., David Kier, Tim Ropes, Deborah Wright, and Sandra Leicester, guerrillas all, made valuable suggestions, which we followed.

*Guerrilla
Selling*

Your Briefing

It's a jungle out there.

No. It's even wilder.

Business in America has changed and continues to evolve so rapidly that even the most sophisticated entrepreneurs have trouble keeping up. Computers, modems, cellular phones, and fax machines have accelerated transactions to the speed of light. Fiber optics and satellites have made the global village economy a reality, and everyone from the Japanese to the Brazilians has invaded and seized markets where America once ruled supreme.

The standard sales techniques of the seventies and eighties are no longer effective. Increased competition and cutthroat pricing demand a higher level of skill and commitment. They demand unconventional weapons and tactics. The new soldiers of fortune must do the unexpected if they are to stand out in a world of carbon-copy products and services.

Fortunately, staying ahead of the pack is easier if you're a guerrilla. New brain research has provided the selling equivalent of night-vision scopes and laser-guided missiles. You may have to rethink your approach by doing the absolute *last* thing your prospect (or your competitors) would expect.

Guerrilla selling means breaking with convention, using *time, energy,* and *imagination* instead of brute persuasive force. It means getting to know your customers so well that they *refuse* to do business with anyone else. It means being super honest, super ethical, and super responsive. It means the customer, *not the salesperson,* makes the major decisions about what gets sold and how they want to buy it. It means solving the customers' problems and enlisting them as allies.

A small company in Tennessee manufactures screen-printed advertising specialties: hats, coffee mugs, the kind of stuff the Koreans make for one third the cost. How do they even hope to compete? They obstinately *refuse* to honor a sacred industry tradition. With the distributor's support, they contact the customer directly to expedite the order, helping with artwork, color selection, drop shipments, and other special arrangements. They let the *distributor* worry about net pricing, terms, and paperwork.

And what do the distributors think about having a manufacturer work directly with their customers? They *love* it. Nobody else in the industry gives them that kind of fast, dependable *service*. Nobody in their right mind would dare usurp that hands-off-my-client industry tradition. That's guerrilla selling.

Guerrilla selling takes advantage of recent breakthroughs in the field of psychology. It treats each potential customer as unique and special, then matches its tactics to the individual personality. Although findings have revealed that there are, generally, seven identifiable personality types, a salesperson encounters three of these types most frequently. Because these types can be identified in *less than a minute*, the sales presentation can now be tailored to individual prospects, targeting their needs and motivations with surgical precision. Now the guerrilla can appeal to each prospect's dominant motives, following the most direct route to a buying decision.

Guerrillas move through their territory with complete confidence because they know their way around. They have "friends in low places" who feed them vital *information*, and they use the tactical advantage of *surprise*. Armed with the latest technology, they stalk their competition from *outside* the corporate corridors. They will call on *anyone*. They are in control at all times, using subconscious messages to build deep rapport, trust, and respect in the minds of their clients.

Such tactics *must* be employed in the modern battle for the business high ground. To survive in the new selling environment, whether you sell products or services, you must exercise the ingenuity and boldness of a veteran mercenary. You must become a guerrilla.

1
A Revolutionary Selling System

A guerrilla goes on patrol

Today Bob Miller's business relies on the two most powerful weapons in guerrilla selling: *information* and *surprise*. He never makes a call without a referral, he never uses visual aids, he lets the prospect control the interview, and when the prospect asks him to write up the order, he objects! He's a fanatic about quality and a maniac about service. He's a member of an elite corps of salespeople. Bob is a guerrilla.

He had always dreamed of being a successful businessman, but fresh out of college he had no real experience, no capital, and no business training. Graduating with a degree in engineering, he had a particular interest in assembly methods, but one after another of the big companies turned him down for a job. That made him angry. So he decided to take them on and beat them at their own game. He decided to be his own salesman. Without knowing it, he decided to become a guerrilla.

Unsure where to begin, he drives out to the industrial park to research the market. He talks to receptionists. He talks to the guys who unload the trucks. He talks to shift workers eating their lunch on the lawn. He talks to everyone. He asks lots of questions: What kind of business is this? What do they manufacture? How many do they make? Who does the assembly? Why do they do it that way? Where do they buy from? Who do they sell to? How's business? What problems have they experienced? Who should I talk to about that?

The next morning, he shows up at the loading dock at Corzex Electronics with a box of doughnuts. "I was wondering if you could help me out?" he asks. "Do you know anyone who has recently landed a substantial production contract? Someone who might need contract assembly?" The shipping clerk is particularly helpful. Miller fills several pages of a wire-bound notebook with names and phone numbers, facts and figures.

After three days of cruising around and gathering information, he's ready to make his *first* real sales call.

The first phone contact

Ring, ring. "Hello. Infrared Technologies."

"Hello, is this Linda?" he asks.

"Yes."

"Hi, Linda. I was talking to Connie over at Corzex across the street, and she suggested I give you a call. I was wondering if you could help me out."

"That depends, what are you *selling?*" Her tone makes it sound as if he's doing something illegal.

"I was hoping I could get some advice. Your firm was recommended to me by several people."

Now, using the information he picked up from a shipping clerk, "Could you tell me who's in charge of the assembly of the IT-350?"

"Well, that would be Mr. Carlson."

"Is that Tom Carlson?" he probes.

"No. His name is David. He's the production manager and one of the partners," she explains.

Miller makes some notes and continues, "The reason I ask is that I have some questions about assembly methods I'd like to address to Mr. Carlson. Can you confirm your address for me?"

"Sure."

"I have: 1234 Industrial Parkway, Anytown, USA 23456. Is that correct?"

"Yes it is."

"Better yet, I'll be in the area day after tomorrow. Would you please leave a message for him and let him know I'll stop by?"

"And what was your name?"

"Miller. Bob Miller."

"I'll tell him you called."

"Thank you, Linda. I really appreciate your help."

Now he takes a thank-you note and mails it to Infrared Technologies, 1234 Industrial Parkway, Anytown, USA 23456, *Attention Linda*, thanking her for her help on the phone. He knows she'll get the card even without her last name because *everyone* knows who Linda is.

The first office call

Two days later, dressed casually, without an appointment, he drops in to see the production manager. He greets the receptionist in the foyer. "Hi. You must be Linda?" he says, extending his hand.

"Why, yes, I am."

"I'm Bob Miller. Did you get my card?"

"Yes, I did! Thank you!"

"I just wanted to tell you how much I appreciate your help. I came by hoping I could speak to David. Is he in?"

"Sure. I'll tell him you're here."

A few minutes later, "Hello, Mr. Carlson. My name is Bob Miller. Thanks for taking some time to see me. I have a few questions I'd like to ask about your assembly methods. Do you have a few minutes?"

"Sure, fire away. Would you like some coffee first?"

Carlson's demeanor, body language, and conversational tone quickly tell Miller what he needs to do to get results with this pleasant but possibly indecisive personality. "Sure. I'd love a cup. Black, thank you. Can I sit here?"

"Sure. Make yourself at home."

"For starters, what's your biggest frustration with your assembly line?"

"Why do you ask?" Carlson says, handing Miller the coffee.

"Well, I think I might have a terrific idea for you."

"Okay, I'll tell you one frustration I have. Our demand is seasonal. We don't really have an assembly line. It's too expensive to keep a crew on the payroll full-time."

"What you're saying sounds important. Do you mind if I take some notes? Could I borrow a few sheets of paper, and, uh, something to write with?" Carlson hands him a legal pad and his gold Cross pen.

More information gathering

Filtering the information that he has received from his confidants, Miller asks his first real question. "You must mean seasonal demand for the new IT-350 portable infrared camera," he says. "Can you tell me about the problems you've been having with that?"

"You're familiar with the 350?"

"Not really, but I'd like to see one. Do you have one you could show me?" With that, the production manager demonstrates the new camera, explaining its technical innovations and targeted markets. It's used primarily by construction crews to isolate faults in the roofs of commercial buildings. Bob asks more questions.

Then Carlson shows Bob through the assembly area, explaining how the cameras are built, step by step. The assembly room is meticulously clean, and everything is neatly organized and clearly labeled. Bob takes special notice of a set of schematics hanging on the wall, keeps asking questions, and listens carefully to the answers.

"Do your solder joints hold up under the rough handling this unit would typically get on a construction site? Wouldn't they hold up better if they were done by hand?"

"Yes, they probably would, and I wish we could afford to do it that way. What we really need is someone who could do that kind of custom work on demand." (Ta da!)

Resisting the temptation to solve Carlson's problem, Miller asks another question.

"What kind of warranty is standard in your industry?"

"Usually three years."

"With that kind of warranty, you must do a lot of warranty repairs. How much does it cost to rebuild one of your cameras after it's failed?" Miller asks.

"That's easy. All the electronic components are mounted on a single circuit board, so we just swap out the whole board. The real expense isn't in fixing the cameras; it's the damage it does to our reputation. In fact, we've got a bunch of boards sitting on the repair bench that we haven't had time to rebuild."

"In round numbers, how much does it cost for each rebuild?"

"Well, they're easy to repair. We could budget fifty dollars each and still be money ahead."

"If you could buy the boards as a complete subassembly, approximately how many a month would you need?"

"We're shipping about two hundred finished cameras a month, and we're still back-ordered. Our big risk is that we could develop a reputation for poor service."

Later, after several more questions . . .

"So, if I understand you correctly, David, you really need a subcontractor who will do a fair amount of the development work, who really cares about quality, and who will share the risk up-front. Isn't that what you're saying?" Bob asks. "Who else, besides yourself, would be involved in making a commitment like that?"

Because of the many questions he'd asked, Carlson can see that Bob has a thorough understanding of his needs. "Tell me, Bob, about *your* firm."

The presentation

Bob responds with one of several well-rehearsed presentations about his new business. This friendly approach is designed for Carlson's unique personality type.

"The truth is that Miller Research is a very new firm, and I'd really appreciate any suggestions you could offer. By doing the critical solder joints by hand and testing everything three times, I'm absolutely confident that we can reduce your failure rate. By distributing some of the payroll costs to a subcontractor, you are relieved of the risk of having a large assembly crew sitting idle during the seasonal sales slump. And your customers will stop cursing camera failures in the middle of their important contracts."

"Sounds good to me," Carlson interrupts.

The guerrilla objects

"Well, something's still bothering me," Miller continues. "You said you needed someone totally reliable, and I'm a newcomer. I'll need some of your time and a lot of your input to get set up for this. Because you'd be one of our first customers, you'd have complete control over the schedules and standards. Is that going to be okay?"

Carlson decides to act on faith. Something about this young man impresses him. Perhaps it's his genuine interest and honest concern. He decides to trust his instincts.

"How soon could you get started on an order of, say, a hundred units?" he asks.

"How soon do you need them?" is Miller's reply.

"By the end of the month."

"There's another problem. I'll have to raise enough money to buy an inventory of parts, and I'll have to set up a dedicated assembly area.

That will take a few days. You might not want to do business with a subcontractor that was a complete start-up. Let me ask, on a scale of one to ten, how confident do you feel doing business with us?"

"Well, Bob, I'd say about seven or so!" Carlson says with a smile.

"What would you need in order to get to ten?" Miller asks.

"I'd need to see what kind of work you do on the first hundred boards. We can get you started with the parts we have on hand, and can pay for 25 percent of the order in advance. Let's see what you can do for us."

And a reward

"You've made a good decision, Dave, thank you for your confidence," Bob says, standing to leave.

With that commitment in hand, he rents a small warehouse space a few doors down from Infrared Technologies and launches his firm. The next morning, in a Federal Express envelope, Mr. Carlson finds a brief letter of intent and a thank-you card. Inside are two tickets to that week's basketball game. Over the next few weeks, Bob Miller is in constant contact with his new customer, and Dave Carlson spends a lot of time at Miller Research as well.

The new guerrilla

Without a brochure, without a business card, without even a briefcase, our new guerrilla walked out with a substantial order and a client that was ultimately worth several hundred thousand dollars to Miller's firm. Today Bob Miller's company builds everything from robots to lasers. He still makes his sales calls in jeans, and he never carries a briefcase, or even a pen. His guerrilla approach has made him a contender in a crowded field where cutthroat pricing and offshore competition are the norm. His customers wouldn't consider sending their work anywhere else.

Was he just lucky? Not at all. His prospecting, his analysis, and even his presentation were all carefully planned, and he's been "lucky" with those same tactics again and again.

Miller's story isn't unique. It's been repeated again and again in firms large and small, from Apple Computer to Xerox, by the renegade who sneaks in and, against all odds, gets the business. Guerrilla selling comes naturally to the neophyte. That's why a new recruit often outperforms the veteran during the first few months in the field. Unfortunately, naive enthusiasm and questioning are soon replaced by the corporate party line as the recruit gets all the facts, memorizes the standard pitch, stops asking, starts closing, and stops selling.

NaB & CaPTuRe

Now let's take a closer look at exactly how Bob used *information* and *surprise* to capture his first contract. Information means learning as much as possible about the prospect's *needs, budget,* and *ability to make a commitment.* Surprise means doing the *unusual,* the *unexpected,* personalizing the presentation, giving the prospect control, and objecting to the prospect's buying signals.

The consonants in the two words "NaB" and "CaPTuRe" guide you in the stages of a guerrilla sale.

Information
1. Need
2. Budget
3. Commitment

Surprise
4. Presentation
5. Transaction
6. Reward

Bob began by using one of several guerrilla prospecting techniques called "Friends in Low Places." By taking time to get to know people involved in the industry, he could gather useful intelligence.

Bob turned a gatekeeper receptionist from an adversary into an ally by enlisting her help, asking her to provide additional information. Consequently, Bob was able to open the conversation with Mr. Carlson by asking informed questions in a helpful way. By asking about the problems with the IT-350, he gained immediate credibility and allowed Carlson to show off his new product.

The guerrilla sale began with the *Need Stage,* asking questions to find out what the prospect needs or wants to buy before beginning any presentation. This allowed Bob to qualify his prospect at the very start and to *weed out nonbuyers quickly.* This Need Stage required him to ask open-ended questions to uncover key issues, and to carefully observe his prospect's behavior.

During this stage, Carlson painted a clear picture of his wants and needs. The clearer the picture, the more our guerrilla is able to satisfy those needs.

Like most prospects, David Carlson required a lot of assistance to see his priorities clearly. Bob assisted this process by *asking questions and by* NOT *giving any answers.* In this stage, he tried to say as little as possible and *encouraged his prospect to talk.* He saved his good news for the Presentation Stage where it wrapped up the sale. When he had a clear idea of the product or service he could sell to fill that need, he moved on to the *Budget Stage.*

In the Budget Stage, he found out if his prospect could *pay* for the service. This stage also required a lot of questions. Some prospects are reluctant to tell a salesperson specific dollar amounts, but Bob overcame this reluctance by asking *"approximately"* and *"in round numbers."*

Bob's next step was to establish a budget based on the *potential* cost of ongoing quality and service problems, rather than the *actual* cost of building the camera's circuit boards. This justifies the higher price of using an outside contractor by protecting the company's most critical asset: its reputation. This cost-benefit justification can be used later in the Presentation Stage if necessary. By using the *potential cost* approach, rather than selling on price, Bob changes the arena of competition and virtually eliminates cheaper vendors from the running. If there's an adequate budget, he moves on to the *Commitment Stage.*

The Commitment Stage is where he discovers who has the necessary *authority* and *when* the prospect will be able to make a buying commitment. Bob knew it was time to move on when the prospect asked, "How soon could you get started on an order of, say, one hundred units?" in effect, offering a commitment.

Our guerrilla also confirms the key criteria for the sale: "So, if I understand you correctly, you need . . ." in effect, closing the sale before the presentation. He has to listen very closely and take careful notes at this phase. The answer to each question provides additional information needed to complete the picture. If he can deliver on these key criteria, he can make the sale, and he can safely ignore everything else.

At the conclusion of the first three stages Bob knew:

1. This prospect had a *need* that he could satisfy.
2. This prospect had a sufficient *budget* allocated for this expense.
3. This prospect could *commit* to buy today.

Now he was ready to begin the *Presentation Stage*. This presentation clearly shows how well Bob's contract assembly service will fill this prospect's priorities and criteria by relieving him of the financial burden of a trained assembly crew and improving the durability of the cameras.

At the Presentation Stage, Bob offered *only* those facts that were relevant to the concerns that the production manager had expressed: quality and availability of help (without having a full-time crew of his own). In addition, he invited Carlson to participate in customizing the service setup so that he could get exactly what he wanted. Bob tailored his approach and style to his prospect's personality, and the prospect became convinced to buy, based on his feelings. Bob knew that being included in *every* aspect of the transaction was a primary motivator for this prospect. That's what Dave Carlson was feeling when he decided he could trust this young man. Because Carlson had a primarily *Pleaser* type personality, Bob knew that Dave was anxious to avoid the wrath of his disappointed customers.

The guerrilla then began the *Transaction Stage*. During this critical maneuver, Bob retraced his steps *back to a minor problem* raised earlier, reminding his prospect that he was a newcomer, lacked a parts inventory, and needed to fund his start-up. This gave his prospect the opportunity to resell himself and ensured against buyer's remorse. In fact, when asked about writing up the order, this guerrilla objected! The prospect actually overcame these potential objections for him.

Since the prospect had already decided that he wanted to do business, he participated in collaborative problem solving and offered our guerrilla more advantageous terms than he would have sought for himself. Because the order for the first hundred circuit boards was the prospect's idea, he will not regret the decision later.

Then Bob moved to the *Reward Stage*, when he expressed his genuine appreciation for the business and did something extra, something out of the ordinary, exceeding his customer's expectations, sending the thank-you note and tickets to the basketball game.

Continued recon: tracking

All guerrillas depend on good reconnaissance, and from that day forward, Bob *tracked* his customer very carefully. A sale is never complete until the product or service is delivered in such a manner that *the customer will order again and again*. He made sure the first order of one hundred boards was delivered *exactly* on time and met *all* the customer's specifications. By tracking his statistics on failure rates, he can monitor his quality and be certain that the original problem raised by the production manager has been solved once and for all.

Now he's first in line the next time there's a production snag at Infrared Technologies, in effect, *closing the sale before he opens it*. Soon they'll have additional needs requiring an updated product or more extensive services. Responding to customer priorities is critical to Bob's long-term success, and Infrared Technologies depends on him to deliver consistently. Guerrillas build long-term customer confidence and return to sell them over and over again.

A nine-word credo for guerrillas

Nine characteristics are shared by guerrillas all over the world. They're easy to remember because each word ends in "ent." Memorize them. Live by them.

1. Commitment

Guerrillas are deadly serious about serving customers, making money, and building a future for themselves and their companies. They do not see selling as a career steppingstone, but as one of the most demanding and highly paid professions. When they lose business to a competitor, they hunt down the cause and correct it. They will risk everything except quality, and they treat every account as if their business depends on it, because it does.

If you're not 100 percent committed to your customers, your product, and your organization, you'll never survive as a guerrilla. If it's your own business and you'd rather work on research and development or operations, hire someone who is totally committed to your customers' needs and make that person your designated guerrilla.

2. Investment

Guerrillas invest time, energy, and money in deployment. They know that they can't win the battle if their ammunition is obsolete. Buy the most current mailing lists, the most expensive directories, and the very best office and communications equipment you can get. Don't skimp on your letterheads and stationery. Go first class. If your company doesn't provide business cards, print them yourself, by the thousands.

Yes, it sounds difficult. Planning and researching your market, your competitors, and your prospects take valuable time. And it often seems like a waste, calling on the same people again and again, being turned down over and over. But the time and money you invest in those relationships is a smart investment in the long run, if you manage them carefully. Be on the lookout for opportunities to leverage your selling capital for a greater return. For example, can the prospect give you an introduction to another company, a referral, or a testimonial letter, as well as an order?

Rewarding customers for doing business with you is a particularly conservative investment. Don't expect overnight miracles. You might not hear from them again for months. But just like your blue-chip stocks, years from now they'll be worth a fortune.

The average business in America invests only 3 percent of gross sales in marketing. The guerrilla averages 10 percent. Reinvest 10 percent of your commissions in your customers and you'll leave the competition in the dust.

And do something every day to invest in yourself. Constantly improve your knowledge of the product, the market, and the customer. Subscribe to and read the trade journals that serve your industry. We recommend *Inc.*, *Personal Selling Power*, and *Success* magazines. Ask yourself, "What could I improve?" Ask your customers. Listen to their answers. Act on them. Organize focus groups of customers and ask, "How are we doing?" If you really listen, your customers will tell you *exactly* what you must do to succeed.

3. Consistent

Poor selling done consistently will be more effective than great selling done sporadically. The guerrilla who is *consistent* will outsell the better armed, better equipped, better organized corporate regulars, because prospects will trust them.

In the mind of the prospect, consistency is interpreted as credibility, longevity, and success. This creates a feeling of trust. Guerrillas earn the confidence of their prospects, and soon prospects become customers.

Most buying decisions are made unconsciously, and psychology has shown us how to reach into the unconscious mind of prospects: *repetition is the key.* At the risk of repeating ourselves, we'll say that again: repetition.

Repetition is required on two fronts: selling the message to prospects and selling the message to the sales staff. Guerrillas repeat their offer to the same people over and over again. Even when prospects say no, and particularly when they say yes. They repeat their presentations and their specials and their seasonal offers. They repeat their message and their benefits.

And they repeat their sales training routinely. Weekly. Daily. *Constantly.* The most successful sales organizations in the world train and train and retrain. They train the truck drivers and the telephone receptionists and the service techs. Everyone hears the company's unique mission and values echoed in meetings, in the hallway, in the cafeteria, on posters in the rest rooms.

Repetition. It's how the world knows who you are and what you're about. By maintaining the same *identity* over time, guerrillas attract business the others have left behind in their hasty charge.

Do not capriciously change your prices, your products, or your guerrilla approach. Just about the time you're bored stiff with your products, your presentation, and your proposal, the community you serve is just getting to know you and associating your name with its needs. By being consistent, guerrillas become the *second* most likely source for their prospects, and when the competition screws up, they automatically inherit those customers.

Lee Iacocca started as a salesman for Ford, and part of the reason he's made Chrysler so successful is that he still sees his job the same way: he's selling cars.

4. Confident

Guerrillas know that they're selling *quality.* Unless your offering is top quality, guerrilla selling will only accelerate your demise. Guerrillas believe in their *products* and their *people.* They depend on the rest of the organization to deliver on every promise, every time, and then some. If they can't feel that kind of absolute trust, they're working for the wrong outfit. They *never* bad-mouth anyone, even the competition. When something goes wrong, they take *personal* responsibility.

In an exit-poll survey, 10,000 shoppers in fifty states were asked,

"Why did you buy that item *here?*" Of their responses, "selection" ranked fourth, after third-ranked "service." Only 14 percent said price was most important; it ranked ninth overall. The second most frequent answer was "quality."

At the *top* of the list, ranked as the most frequently cited reason for buying from a particular store, was "confidence." They felt confident that their needs would be met and the dealer would stand behind its products. Guerrillas do *everything* they can to communicate their own absolute confidence in their company, their offering, and themselves. That confidence spreads to prospects and customers.

5. Patient

Customers may not need your offering today, but they will sooner or later. Needs are cyclical. For example, if you've just eaten a big meal, you don't feel much like having a pizza. Your appetite has been sated, for the time being. But in a few hours, you'll begin to feel hungry again. Guerrillas are always on the lookout for the next *need cycle*, and strive to be there when the need arises. They *keep* calling long after the competition has moved out and moved on.

Less than 4 percent of sales are made on the first call; *over 80 percent are made after the eighth call.* So the guerrilla sticks with it, getting some additional buying commitment on each call. On average it requires at least *nine impressions* of your company, your product, or your idea to move the mind of a prospect from total apathy to purchase readiness. To develop a major new account may take *months.*

6. Assortment

Guerrillas offer a wide variety of goods and services, and can adapt their offering, their terms, even their delivery schedule to meet customers' needs. The more flexible they can be, the better. The old days of Henry Ford, when "you can have it any color you want, as long as it's black" are long gone. The more options you offer, the more people you can serve, and the more you can sell. But guerrillas also *stick to what they do well* and sell what they do *best.*

7. Subsequent

Guerrillas succeed by fighting for successive sales, and concentrate most of their efforts selling to existing accounts. They wage their sales campaigns simultaneously on three fronts: the *Universe*, their *Prospects*, and their *Customers*. Guerrillas marshal their resources to concentrate primarily on the third group.

The first arena, the *Universe*, includes everyone in their service area. Everyone.

Guerrillas invest 10 percent of their selling time reaching out to this massive audience, at random, getting out the message, establishing their identity in the marketplace. They strike up conversations with people on airplanes and commuter trains (more on this in the next chapter). They get themselves interviewed on radio talk shows. They leave stacks of business cards on the counter by the cash register in the restaurant where they eat lunch. People who have an embryonic interest will pick them up and move into the next sphere.

The next group is smaller, a subset of the first, and includes all *Prospects*.

Guerrillas know that someone is a prospect if they have a potential need for their offering, now or in the future. They needn't have met. They're not in the guerrilla's file box, *yet*. Guerrillas devote 30 percent of their selling time to *Prospects* by letting them know that they exist and gathering as much information about them as possible.

Harvey Mackay, author of the best seller *Swim With the Sharks Without Being Eaten Alive*, shares the secret of his successful envelope

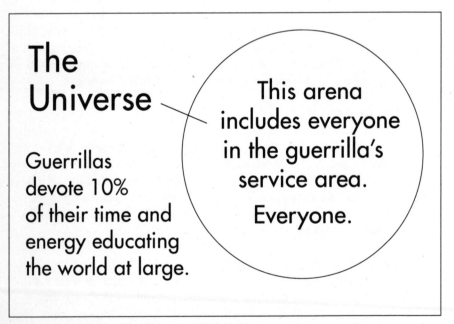

The Universe

Guerrillas devote 10% of their time and energy educating the world at large.

This arena includes everyone in the guerrilla's service area.

Everyone.

Fig. 1.1

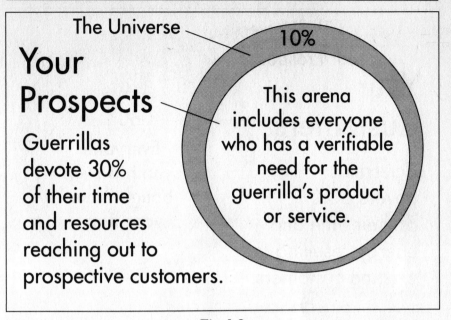

The Universe

Your Prospects

Guerrillas devote 30% of their time and resources reaching out to prospective customers.

10%

This arena includes everyone who has a verifiable need for the guerrilla's product or service.

Fig. 1.2

business: his salespeople have a questionnaire of sixty-six items of interest on *every* prospect. The form doesn't include only business questions. Mackay's people find out your kids' names, church affiliation, even favorite sports teams, and they use this information to build a close human bond.

The third domain is the smallest, at the core of the other two, and includes all your *Customers*.

This includes everyone who has purchased anything from your company, ever. *Guerrillas invest 60 percent of their selling time reaching out to people who have already bought.* Yes, it's unconventional. That's why it works. Existing customers are the most likely source of referral business, and the only source of repeat sales. The smallest group should have the *most* time spent on it.

Guerrillas are in this for *the lifetime value* of a customer. For example, a shopper spends about $100 a week in the grocery store, and on any Saturday the store is crawling with customers. So what if someone gets upset and goes somewhere else? Who cares? For the guerrilla, that's the $1,500 question, because $100 a week, fifty weeks a year, over the ten years a customer shops in that store, is a lot of groceries.

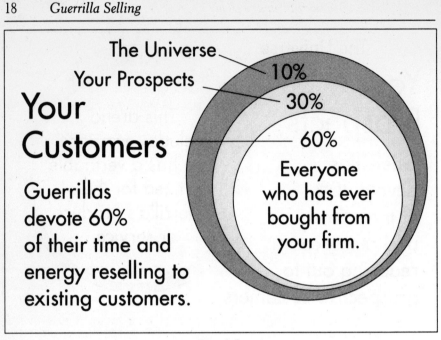

The Universe
Your Prospects
10%
30%
Your Customers — 60%

Everyone who has ever bought from your firm.

Guerrillas devote 60% of their time and energy reselling to existing customers.

Fig. 1.3

Assume a profit margin of only 3 percent, and that's $1,500 in pure profit walking out the door. If someone stole $1,500 from your cash register, you'd be fuming.

Let's look at some *really* interesting numbers. If someone has a good experience with your company, they'll tell three people. If they have a bad experience, they'll tell *twenty*. Word of mouth is one of the most potent weapons in the guerrilla arsenal. Guerrillas use it with great care to build and protect a reputation for service, quality, and excellence.

8. Convenient

Guerrillas know that they have to be *buyer friendly*. They have to be easy to reach, easy to talk to, and easy to do business with. They answer their own phone. They return their own calls. They give out their numbers at home, at the office, in the car, and carry a pager. They have the phones manned at night and on weekends, even if only by an answering service. They are in touch.

A true guerrilla would never hand the customer an order form to fill out. They *take care of all of the paperwork* themselves. They *do everything immediately*.

9. Excitement

Guerrillas are enthusiastic. They have a good word for everyone. They are *militantly* optimistic. They *never* complain about the weather, the economy, or the people they work for. Their passion spreads like wildfire. People love to do business with people who love their business.

These are the characteristics that guide the guerrilla's field tactics. They protect him from detection and assault. Post these nine "ents" on the dashboard of your car. Sell by them. Live by them.

Now you've seen how a guerrilla secures a sales without the traditional "pitch." You've seen an overview of how to NaB & CaPTuRe prospects once you've gotten an appointment. In the following chapters, you'll learn about unconventional sources of prospective customers, how to zero in on their needs, priorities, and criteria, and you'll see how to deploy your selling arsenal for an almost certain victory.

Good hunting, future guerrilla. Remember that your prospects, your clients, and your customers are all allies. Your foe is ignorance of your prospects' real needs. To a guerrilla salesperson, the competition doesn't stand a chance.

2
Guerrilla Prospecting

The cold call

Traditionally, cold-call prospecting meant talk to as many people as possible, ignore the turndowns, and close, close, close.

"Good morning, Mr. Jones, this is Jim Smith with Acme Distribution."

"Uh-huh."

"We sell . . . which are the finest . . . and they . . . (minutes later) So, I'm calling you today to ask you . . ."

"Zzzzzz . . ."

The guerrilla turns this traditional approach around and *gets the prospect to ask the questions,* listens to the answers, and then asks for a sales appointment. How?

"Hello, Mr. Jones? Do you know why I'm calling you today?"

"No, I don't."

"Hmmm, I have a memo here asking me to give you a call, and I was hoping that you could tell me what it was about?"

"What was the name of your company again?"

"Acme Distribution."

"What do you sell?"

"I'm not surprised you asked. We sell . . ."

Instead of charging toward the prospect head-on with fixed bayonet, the guerrilla takes a hide-in-the-trees-and-take-a-clear-shot approach to prospecting. Most salespeople fall into habitual patterns based on what's worked for them over the years, and sales managers often depend solely on the classic selling texts. But the buying public has become more sophisticated and more demanding. They've seen the same show, and they know exactly what's coming next. They resent being treated according to the same tired formulas. Everyone has the same thing to say, and any possible competitive advantage is lost.

But not the guerrilla. The note from his boss said something like, "John, call everybody on this page and tell them about our new line." Guerrillas create curiosity from the first sentence. Then they convert that curiosity into interest and warm that interest into appointments. The keys to guerrilla prospecting are *information* and *surprise*.

A million-dollar guerrilla

Australian guerrilla Geof Cook sells commercial life and casualty insurance, and writes over a million dollars in premiums every year by ambushing Gold Coast real estate offices.

In sandals and beachwear, he strolls into an office and strikes up a conversation with the receptionist. The front-desk staff are told that all walk-ins could be prospects, so his inquiries about the state of business, the quality of housing in the area, and the principals' names are all answered directly. If possible, he asks to see the broker.

Here he shifts into a disarming conversation about market prices and movements, gently probing and warming the broker's attitude. One of the questions he asks is "What is the *one* thing you find *most* annoying in running your business?" The usual answer: "All the paperwork at closing."

Then he offers the broker a free service. He volunteers to prepare all the insurance paperwork for the broker whenever a building is sold. In addition, he will issue an interim policy on the property that protects the seller and the agent from liability in the event of damage to the building before the new owner occupies it. And, he adds, his office will issue this temporary coverage for *nothing*.

He only asks that the agent fax him a copy of the signed purchase contract. This document provides all the information — legal description of the real estate, names and addresses of the parties, appraised value of the building, and so on — that Geof needs to prepare the policy.

Then he sends a cover letter with a copy of the policy to the buyers, along with an easy-to-read explanation of the fine print and a proposal explaining how they can continue the required coverage on the building after they move in. All they have to do is sign the last page, and it's done. No-hassles shopping for insurance.

As a courtesy, he also sends copies to the lenders and legal people, saving everyone time and money. This is more service than these people have seen from an insurance agent in ten years.

This tactic puts Geof in touch with new prospects with an immediate need, even before they leave their old neighborhood. More important, he's built a following of loyal brokers who fax him a basketful of new business every day. Combining information and surprise, he's built a million-dollar business.

Planning

Guerrillas *never* go out on maneuvers without planning carefully, because they know it's one of the competition's strategic weaknesses. Have you ever had someone try to sell you something when they were completely unprepared? How did it make you feel? Nothing dampens the enthusiasm to buy like a clerk who fiddles with the knobs and switches, then scratches his head in ignorance. Yet salespeople routinely walk into an important meeting completely unarmed, hoping that they'll somehow wing it. They shoot from the hip, then wonder why they miss the mark.

Planning can help you position your product in the market. Guerrillas carefully aim their offering at a particular niche. Is it a Chevy or a Mercedes? Is it Kmart or Neiman Marcus? It may be defined by geography or by a particular industry. Guerrillas look at the competition and try to position themselves to capture the high ground.

Guerrilla prospecting consists of three parts: finding prospects, approaching them, and securing an appointment. The prospect typically becomes a client when the guerrilla completes the NBC stages of NaB & CaPTuRe. The *Need* is verified, a *Budget* is established, and a buying *Commitment* can be made.

Finding prospects

The old cliche about "selling refrigerators to Eskimos" is an insult to the guerrilla. For them, prospecting is based on the idea that it is easier to find people who *already* want, need, or have to buy your product than it is to convince or persuade or pressure someone who doesn't. They look for obvious needs they can fill. Who is out there that already wants, needs, and has to have your product? A prospect is anyone who meets these three qualifications:

1. They have a *need.*
2. They have a *budget.*
3. They have the authority to make a *commitment.*

Unlimited prospects

One day a young advertising sales rep was sitting at his desk shuffling prospect cards when his manager walked in and asked sharply, "What are you doing here? There are still two hours left in the day. You should be out making *calls!*"

"I've run out of leads," the new salesman responded.

"Hmmm . . . I have a *special list* of companies that I haven't shared with anyone else on the crew. How would you like to work part of this special list?"

"I'd love to!" said the salesman, jumping out of his chair.

The manager reached down, opened the lower left-hand drawer of his desk, and pulled out a thick book. Turning to the back, he ripped out a handful of pages and handed them to the shocked young man.

"The *Yellow Pages?* I thought you said you had a *special* list!"

"That's right, and I don't want to see you in this office again until you've followed up on every one of them."

"But . . ."

"Listen, the phone book is the *last* place most salespeople look, and those who do start in the front. You've got every business there from 'Travel Agencies' to 'Zoos,' and if you can't find *someone* in there who needs advertising, I don't need you."

Flipping through the pages, the rep picked an ad for a van-conversion shop just a few blocks away. The ad listed the name of the business, the address, and the owner's name, plus the types of vans they worked on. He decided to give it a try.

"Hi, I'm looking for Vic Andrews," he said to the man who greeted him as he entered the shop.

"You found him. What can I do for you?"

"I came by because of your ad in the Yellow Pages."

"*Really!*" Vic said with a chuckle. "You're the first person who's said that in years. I was beginning to think that ad was a waste of money."

"How much does an ad like that cost?" the rep asked, as if he didn't already know.

"I pay about a hundred dollars a month."

"Gee, twelve hundred dollars a year! I work in advertising, and that seems like a lot of money to put into an ineffective media. What other advertising do you do?"

"That's about it," Vic said. "Most of my work's off referrals."

Here was a prospect who had been in business for a decade and had relied strictly on his Yellow Pages ad and customer word-of-mouth. Here was someone he could help. With the *Need* and *Budget* now established, he was off and running. Within a month, the new salesman led the company in total sales and nearly doubled the record for new business.

Reconnaissance first

Once you've found a prospect, get ready to do some homework. *Gather as much data in advance as possible.* Any information may prove valuable. We recommend recording your notes on blank three-by-five cards or special sales-prospect cards available from most office supply stores. Your firm may have some other system such as a prospect-record sheet. The most important thing is to record it.

"*Recon*" *is the one big secret to guerrilla prospecting.* The more information you have, the better your chances for making the right approach. This also means regularly shopping your competition, reading their brochures, flyers and catalogs, even memorizing their price lists.

Warming up the cold call

They're called "cold" calls because of the shiver that runs up your spine every time you have to make one. Most salespeople dread cold calls for the same reason: fear of the unknown. Researching your prospects will help you be more confident because *information cures fear.*

Do you remember Neil Armstrong climbing down the ladder of the Apollo 11 lunar lander? Talk about cool! Eight hundred million people are watching on television and he's about to set foot on the moon. A fairly unnerving situation, but not for Neil. He steps on the moon and calmly says, "That's one small step for a man, one giant leap for mankind."

There wasn't anything special about Neil Armstrong, except that *he had spent fifteen years planning that one small step.* He knew everything that there was to know about that ship, every system and every back-up. He'd been through hundreds of exercises and drills. He had far more information than he ever really needed to complete the mission. That's why he was so cool. The more that you know about the situation going in, the less reluctant you'll be.

Building enthusiasm

Information is also a great enthusiasm builder. Think about a subject about which you know little or nothing — like beekeeping or exploring caves. When you take time to learn about these activities, they become much more interesting. No doubt, there are hundreds of people who are enthusiastic about these activities. When you talk to them about their interests, their enthusiasm is contagious. Caught up in their excitement, you listen with interest to stories about how the queen bee signals her daughters, or about stalactites, stalagmites, and flowstone curtains.

To warm up to any product or service, you must first gather information, and with it you will gain confidence *and* enthusiasm. Study until you become an expert. Learn as much as you can about every aspect of your product, your competitors' products, and any other product that could be substituted for your product. Learn about every possible application of your product and every industry that uses it. This expertise will make you more enthusiastic, more confident, and more anxious to tell others. It also makes you more interesting to talk to and more fun to do business with. It's the bunker that protects you from the depression that accompanies occasional failure.

Warm up to your prospects in the same way, by getting to know them ahead of time. If you take a sincere interest in them, they will be much more likely to take an interest in you and your proposition. Use this dig-deeper technique, and you'll never have to make another cold call in your life.

Five steps to finding prospects:

1. Identify your "ideal" prospects, the people who are most likely to buy from you.

Who are they? What do they look like? Where would you find them? When do they need your product? Find out as much as you can about them: their age, gender, income, education, hobbies, community involvement. This is the first step in your intelligence gathering. Ask yourself what responsibilities they have. What problems are they trying to solve? What's their potential motivation for entering into this transaction? Who do they report to? Who reports to them? What are they using now? How much are they paying for it? What do they like most about it? What do they like least about it? Why would they want to improve? And how can you help? With this information, the guerrilla can zero in on the people who have the real buying power. By profiling your ideal prospects, you'll recognize them better when you meet them in the community, on the commuter train, or sit next to them on an airplane.

2. Get out in the field.

Scout around. Go to the best areas you've identified and interview your ideal prospects in shopping malls, business parks, industrial centers, libraries, university campuses, airports, residential neighborhoods, and anywhere else they are likely to be found. What do they do? How do they do it? What problems do they experience? How could your product or service help? This field work is the second part of your recon.

3. Use an unusual, creative, or unexpected approach.

Get prospects on your side, in person or on the phone. Remember, just like you, many people really enjoy helping others. Try the bumbling Columbo method. Ask them, "I was wondering if you could help me out?" Tell people what you're looking for and let them assist.

4. Ask a lot of questions.

We're often so anxious to share the good news about our business that we forget to build trust and confidence. The guerrilla understates the case so the prospects will feel comfortable and invite them to set a sales appointment.

5. Listen actively to the answers.

That means listening to both the *content* and the *emotional* message, really hearing them. The objective is to build trust, to let prospects know that we really care about them and their needs. Stop telling, teaching, explaining, and persuading. Stop selling. There'll be time enough for that later.

Door-to-door revisited

A computer retailer used guerrilla prospecting to substantially increase his traffic. Watch as he follows each of these steps for finding prospects, researching their needs, employing a creative approach, and finally setting up an appointment.

He noticed that many of the people he talked to in the store were parents who were curious about how computers were being used at school. He recognized that they would be ideal prospects for low-cost word processing and other educational computer applications at home.

Having identified this customer profile, *step one*, he started asking every customer in the store if they had children, and if so, where they went to school and whether they had a computer at home.

He took a walk to the nearest high school, *step two*, and talked with several teachers, asking for suggestions and advice on software and gathering a number of endorsements. He then took a walk through the neighborhood. At one house, he stopped to admire a beautiful rose garden. Almost every neighborhood has a house like this one. Inside lives someone who is usually very responsible, someone who has the time to take care of roses, perhaps a retired couple or widow, who knows everyone on the block.

With pen and legal pad poised, he knocked. "Good morning." Handing her his business card, he continued, "I was wondering if you could help me?" *Step three*. "I work for a computer store downtown, and I'm doing a little research on how computers help youngsters do better in school. Could you suggest some families in the area that I might interview?" *Step four.*

"Oh, yes," was the reply. "There are the Davidsons two doors down. They have two very bright children, and then across the street are the Hamiltons. Their boy just won an award in science."

Writing hastily, the salesman said, "Great. His parents must be very proud." In ten minutes he had the scoop on every house on the block, and two or three that looked especially promising. *Step five.* He commented on the home owner's beautiful roses and thanked her profusely for her help.

Referral pipelines

Guerrillas develop *several* pipelines of people who have a natural need for their product or service, or who can help the guerrilla find these people in other ways. A guerrilla is always on the lookout for referrals, and at each stage, attempting to discover more about them.

It helps if people refer you to their friends, associates, and family. This puts you and your prospect on a common ground from the beginning. But remember to look in the unconventional places.

"Good morning, Mrs. Hamilton," says the guerrilla, handing her his card. "I was just across the street speaking with Mrs. Jeffries, and she suggested I speak with you. I want to interview the parents of some students who have shown academic achievement. Is it true that your son recently won an award of some sort?" Always finish with a question.

"Yes. He just won first prize in the science fair."

"I'd like to hear more about that. The company I work for is involved in the use of computers in education, and I have a few questions I'd like to ask you and your husband. It will take about twenty minutes or so. We could meet here or at our store downtown. Where would be better for you, here or at the store?"

"I guess here would be more convenient."

"Would tonight at seven be good, or would tomorrow at noon be better?"

"Seven would be fine."

"Thank you. Please tell your husband that I'll be by at seven."

Now the guerrilla has an appointment, but he doesn't stop here.

Virtually every contact you meet can provide a referral, or useful information of some sort if you ask the right questions.

". . . And perhaps you can help me locate other families like yourselves. I understand the Davidson children are doing quite well in school?"

"I don't know about that," she says. "Mark's a classmate of Tony's and he's more the athletic type."

"Hmmm," he says, writing all this down. "Anyone else?" And so it goes. In two hours, he has three or four appointments with families he has reason to believe have a need.

In this case, we're looking for families who would use a home computer and educational software. We almost always need to talk to both parents to get a decision. If we find out the type of work they do, or take a quick look around the house, or check out the car in the driveway, we can guess a lot about their commitments and ability to buy.

The whole truth

A word of caution: *the truth is one of the most devastating tactics in the guerrilla's arsenal*. It will save you time. When someone asks point-blank, "What are you selling?" don't hedge. Tell them, "I'm selling computers."

"We already have three, so don't waste your time."

"Great!" Now you know two things: first, they're *not* going to buy, and second, they *believe* in the product you represent. Next step: ". . . Then perhaps you could refer me to another educationally minded family in the area who is not quite so fortunate?"

Ask and ye shall receive

In interviewing hundreds of salespeople, we found it interesting that many of them did not bother to ask for referrals from their existing customers, which, when you think about it, is not too guerrilla-like. Guerrillas constantly cultivate their customer list for referrals. The best time to ask for referrals is *immediately after* you've delivered the product or service. There is no better time. But you can ask for a referral at other times too.

Lou Pinder is one of the top distributors in the world for courses produced by Success Motivation Institute. After each sale, he simply turns to a blank page in his legal pad, writes large-sized numerals, one through six, down the left margin, and says, "Just like you, my business depends on meeting people. Would you please give me the names of six others who, like yourself, are interested in becoming more successful?" He sits quietly with an expectant smile, pen poised. He gets six referrals from almost every sale, and because his closing ratio runs about one in five, he almost never makes a cold call.

How to help clients give you referrals

Many salespeople mistake a client's hesitation to refer others as a sign of unwillingness. The problem may simply be that they're thinking more about the new product than they are about possible referrals.

Who do you know who...

A guerrilla selling life insurance in Los Angeles helps clients suggest referrals by asking a simple question: "Who do you know who . . . ?" is the question. The variations run something like:

"Who do you know who was recently promoted?"

"Who do you know who just had a baby?"

"Who do you know who just moved into town?"

"Who do you know who is getting married sometime soon?"

This line of questioning helps your clients recall people who would be good prospects. Formulate the questions so that they ask about people who typically buy your product or service. Even if they don't know someone who is getting married, your question may remind them of someone who just had a wedding anniversary who might be in the market for some additional family protection. The guerrilla lists any names volunteered by the new customer.

Barbershop prospecting

A barber in Detroit has a sign on the wall. "Ask me to explain how you can make $25." The barber tells his customers that if they refer a friend to a particular car dealer, and the referral eventually buys a car, the dealer will pay them $25. He then gives them ten of the dealers' cards and puts their name and phone number on the back. The barber gets a buck for every card he gives out. This dealer outsold every other dealership in the United States, several years running.

A referral tip

A computer salesperson jots a short thank-you note on the back of one of her business cards, leaving it *with her gratuity* whenever she eats out. She's discovered that waiters and waitresses meet a lot of business people, and she's been introduced to several large accounts this way.

The treasure chest

After you've gathered some information, don't let it get scattered and lost. Keep some sort of organized information system for tracking prospects. Simple is better. Staple that business card they gave you to a three-by-five file card and put it in a recipe box. Arrange the box with two sets of divider tabs from an office supply store, one set for the months labeled *JAN* through *DEC*, and another labeled one through thirty-one, for the days of the month, then file the leads chronologically by planned call-back date, placing today's calls in the front, and roll them over daily. Each day begins with a new handful of cards, the guerrilla's calls for that day.

Now when the secretary says, "Mr. Buyer is out of town until Tuesday," you can respond with, "Would you please tell him to expect my call on Wednesday." Refile the card under the appropriate tab, and take your clear shot when the timing is right.

Likewise, people who do not have a need *today* may *develop* one in a month or a year. Use the roll-over technique to make sure you're talking to the right people at the right time. More on this in chapter 11, "Guerrilla Tracking," but you should touch base with every past and current customer at least quarterly, whether they buy or not. Maintain the human bond. Talk about their favorite ball team, or how the kids are doing in school, or how their new location is working out for them. Most important, keep the calls on a personal basis, rather than just business. If you maintain the person-to-person relationship, the business relationship will take care of itself. Keeping in close contact with prospects and clients is a key to business survival.

The guerrilla M-16

Use modern guerrilla weapons if you have them. A computer database or lead-management system can save a lot of time, but it can also overcomplicate your prospecting. If you automate your system, set it up on a portable that you can carry in the field. More on this in chapter 12. Guerrillas not only gather information, but they also organize and manipulate it to their advantage.

Old customers, new business

Patrick McConnell is a guerrilla who sells yachts in San Diego. For years he kept a deck of three-by-five index cards in his pocket. He said to every customer, "I'm just going to make some notes here so the next time we talk I can offer you this boat at the same price or better, okay?" He wrote down the model, the price, serial numbers, and any other pertinent information. He also recorded the prospect's full name and address and asked for the phone number.

He still maintains a file box of everyone he talks to, and another for every boat he's offered. Then, when an owner reduces the asking price, he calls every prospect that has looked at that boat, or a similar model, and invites them to the marina for a second look. Eight out of ten are at the "still just looking" stage, but the second look, or the special price, may be just enough to close the deal.

This broker knows the guerrilla marketing principle that *one of the best sources of new customers is old customers.* For example, when he has an especially beautiful boat to sell, he calls everyone he's sold anything to in the last seven years, knowing that sailors will often trade up if they're offered something unique or special.

Once, when his brokerage firm picked up a new line of smaller sailboats, he rummaged through the shop files, pulling the file-copy invoice for every customer, going back thirteen years. "You will not believe your ears!" he said on the phone as he described the virtues of the new, smaller Catalinas. Many of these customers upgraded their older boats to better-quality, safer equipment. The result: he sold over a hundred of them, two million dollars in ten months.

He also follows up on powerboat buyers, offering them ship-to-shore radios, Fathometers, and Knotmeters, free. This service approach makes him memorable and results in considerable referral business.

It's frustrating for the other salespeople in the firm who stand around, waiting for their next "up," only to have three or four customers in a row come in and ask for Patrick by name. Of the scores of yacht brokers in San Diego selling the same boats, this guerrilla outsells them all. He single-handedly produces as much dollar volume as any ten other salespeople combined.

Unconventional sources of prospect information

A trip to your local business library will be time well spent. Investigate the trade journals that serve your target industry. Read the ads. Look for feature articles about the movers and shakers. Then go to directories like the Dun & Bradstreet *Million Dollar Directory* or *MacRae's Blue Book*.[1] These volumes will provide basic information, like the name and address of every business in a particular area. They can tell you whether it's a home office, a regional office, or a branch office. You can find the name of the purchasing agent, production manager, and other key people. You can even look up their credit rating. That's critical intelligence to have if you are going in to try to close an $80,000 deal, and discover that you won't get it financed because they have a B-4 rating. Guerrillas save the expense of a sales call by qualifying their prospects before they call.

With this basic information, you can call and ask them to mail you a brochure, catalog, or annual report. Guerrillas recon similar companies as well, particularly *their prospects' competitors*, to develop a feel for the entire field. Before entering a new market, they read several months' back issues of the industry's trade journals to get a fix on current trends and to pick up the industry vernacular. It's amazing how dropping a few acronyms can make you look like an insider.

For example, check out the *R. L. Polk City Directory*[2] at the reference desk. This book is divided into four sections. The white section lists every household and every business alphabetically. An "H" in the margin denotes a home owner, and a star in the margin tells us that this entry is new to this year's directory. The yellow section lists businesses by category, like a phone book. The green section lists every home or building at every address by street name and number, and the blue section lists every phone number in numeric order.

---

[1] Available from MacRae's Blue Book, 817 Broadway, New York, N.Y. 10003, or call 212-673-4700.
[2] Better still, order one covering your metropolitan area by calling 313-393-0880.

With this kind of information, a guerrilla might already know the name of the family who lives in that home with the rose garden, as well as information about the companies with the most employees in the community.

Stalking a new prospect

Let's follow a guerrilla who has a note from his boss saying "please call" with a only a phone number scrawled on it. Looking in the blue pages, he finds that the number is listed to one "Consolidated Amalgamated, Inc." Turning to the white pages, under "C," he finds the alpha listing for "Consolidated Amalgamated," along with the address, phone, and a list of the company officers. John Q. Buyer is the president.

Turning now to the yellow section, we find the ad for Consolidated Amalgamated and discover that they're a manufacturing firm, selling foam mattresses for yard furniture. So far, so good.

Back to the white section, under "B," we learn that Mr. Buyer owns his home, is married, his wife's name is Jane, and he has three children. Looking up the address in the green pages, we can find the names and phone numbers of the Buyer family's neighbors as well.

Now let's say that our guerrilla is in the business of selling siding for residential buildings. He can approach the Buyer family confident that they have a genuine need and the economic resources to upgrade their home.

Having sold the Buyers, he then sends a personal letter to every other home owner within a ten-block radius, including a snapshot of the house and inviting them to drive by and take a look at the installation, perhaps touting the savings that the Buyer family will experience, and introducing himself. One sale leads to another, and another, and another, in widening concentric rings throughout the neighborhood.

Dozens of companies produce cross-referenced directories. Investigate them all until you find the ones that work best for your field. Also, consider industry and association directories. If you've been effective penetrating a particular industry, look for other companies of the same stripe. Many associations make their membership directories available for the asking, or for a nominal charge. The Gale *Encyclopedia of Associations* lists over 30,000 national and international groups, and is available at your local library.[3]

[3]Call Gale Publications at 1-800-877-GALE to order your own copy.

Z to A — the guerrilla prospector's alphabet

When working any directory or manufacturer's list, guerrillas begin at the *back* of the book. Every salesman has good intentions when beginning a cold-call program. They enthusiastically start with AAA *Awning* or with *Mr. Aaron*, believing that eventually they'll work their way down to the *Zzyx Zipper Company* or to *Mr. Zimmerman*. It just never happens. Cold calling is not forever. Effective cold callers will soon be working referrals, and the poor cold callers, if they haven't found a way to get out of the directories, will find their way out of selling. It is very likely that Mr. Zimmerman hasn't been called on by *anyone* in a long time!

Extra, extra! Read all about it!

Even the daily newspaper can provide a ready stream of prospects. A New England securities guerrilla scans the daily want ads for people selling big-ticket items. He calls and asks, "I don't mean to be too personal, but if I might ask, what are you planning to do with the money?" He can often suggest high-performance short-term investments where the advertisers can stash the cash while looking for that larger boat, motor home, or vacation cabin. These short-term investors often develop into long-term clients.

Other guerrillas look for feature articles that profile organizations or businesses. The articles usually provide names, titles, and background, but missing details can be quickly researched with a call to the feature writer or editor. They can give you the up-to-date scoop on who's moving and shaking in your community.

Newlyweds

A company in Nebraska imports fine china from Hong Kong and sells it to newly married couples. Because a majority of newlyweds stay in the area where they were married for at least the first few years, guerrillas can retrieve the "Marriage Licenses Issued" column in the newspaper from the library, from six to nine months back. They then call 411 Information for what is likely to be a new phone number. By offering a high-quality product at very moderate prices, the firm is expanding into new markets all over the country.

Centers of influence

In most organizations there are several people who can help you approach your prospect in an informed and innovative manner. Cultivating these relationships will be worthwhile. A *center of influence* is someone influential who has clout with other people. Their name adds credibility and prestige to your offering. If they're your customer, others would like to be too.

Friends in low places

Never underestimate who can help you get the business. Guerrillas know that the only person in the building who has a set of keys that will open every door in the place is the *janitor.* They can tell you the who, what, and where of a prospective company. But they keep owl's hours. Anyone, anywhere can help you find prospective customers, if you ask for help and reward them in some way. Show up on the loading docks at six-thirty in the morning with coffee and fresh doughnuts and talk to the delivery drivers. They'll tell you what is being bought and how much, from whom, when, and the price they're paying.

Gatekeepers

Salespeople often overlook the receptionist or switchboard operator as a potential source of information. Worse yet, they often consider them an obstacle to be overrun in their push to get to the decision maker. Because they control access to the powerful people, they can be *formidable* adversaries, but *they can also be mighty allies*. The guerrilla always treats them with great respect. They often know more about what's going on than the CEO.

Influencers

Many sales involve more than one person: the marketing manager, the chief engineer, a supervisor, or a department head. While not directly responsible for making the final decision, they may substantially affect the outcome. Find out who they are when you are referred to anyone inside a large organization. Make sure you have them on your side before attempting the sale.

The best approach is to ask them for their expert advice. You'll uncover any problems they've had with other suppliers and isolate their key criteria. Remember, what's important to one influencer may seem trivial to another.

Users

In large organizations, remember to talk to the people who will be using the product *before* you make the sales call. You may be able to circumvent them with the first sale, but if they're dissatisfied later on for any reason, your future sales will be foreclosed. The guerrilla talks to them first, asking, "What are you using now? What do you like *most* about it? What do you like *least* about it?" The answers to these questions give the guerrilla the performance specifications for their product or service, revealing the criteria most important in the decision from the user's point of view.

An electric components distributor in Dallas approached a group of assemblers who were eating lunch on the lawn. His questions unearthed a simple complaint: "We get these switches in with five terminals on them, and then we have to stop and cut three of the terminals off before we can use them."

"Yeah, it's really dumb," a young woman added. "They're paying someone to put those terminals on, then paying us to clip them off." The guerrilla brought the problem to the attention of the purchasing agent, proposing a two-terminal switch that was cheaper. He got the order *and* captured the account. If you can win over the civilian population and keep them on your side, the competition will get creamed.

The spy

Guerrillas try to develop a relationship with someone on the inside who can feed them information. This inside spy ideally *should be someone who has your best interests at heart*. It's best if it is someone who would like to see you succeed. But it *must* be ethical.

Friends in high places

The actual decision maker may not be at the top of the totem pole. Bill in Chicago uses a two-call approach to sell long-distance telephone services. He first calls the regional headquarters listed in the phone book and asks for the name and phone number of the president or senior vice presidents of each division in his territory.

He then calls and asks for the office of the head person — president, senior vice president, or regional vice president.

To the big boss he says, "I know I'm talking to the wrong person, but I wonder if you can help me? Who would be the person in charge of handling a telephone analysis?"

"That would be Mr. Traffic Manager."

"Do you think he would be interested in new technology that could reduce long-distance costs?"

"We're always looking for ways to cut costs, but you'll have to talk with him about that."

The second call is to the name supplied by the big boss. "Mr. Traffic Manager? Mr. Big Boss gave me your name and suggested I talk to you about cutting long-distance costs. I understand that you're the one to work with on a telecommunications analysis, and we have some technologies that *Mr. Boss* thought might be of interest to you." With an entree like that, the rest is easy. "The analysis will take less than ten minutes, and I can arrange for someone to come by on Thursday, or would Friday be better?"

"You oughta be in pictures"

A guerrilla stockbroker cuts photos and articles out of the business pages, then mails them to the subject with a brief note: "Congratulations on your promotion! Let me know if I can be of service."

FYI

A guerrilla salesman in Texas clips articles that may be of interest to prospect companies, and sends a copy to the executive as part of a three-step prospecting system. "Enclosed is an article about opportunities in (*topic*). I hope you find it useful." He follows up a few days later with a letter: "I hope you found the article about (*topic*) of interest. Enclosed is a related item that you might find useful." The third letter says, "I'll be in your area on Thursday and would like to meet you. I'll be calling to arrange a mutually convenient appointment." Eight out of ten executives he calls agree to meet their pen pal face-to-face.

Anticipate needs

The guerrilla milkman expands his route by reading the daily birth announcements. When the new mother comes home, she finds the dairy's delivery box sitting on the porch with a card congratulating the family and offering a free gallon of milk each week for a month. Of course, they can call anytime and cancel the service or do nothing and accept this gift. As the baby grows, so does his business, and several of his original gallon-a-week accounts now have several siblings.

Oops!

A guerrilla who leases cars finds prospects by reading the police blotter, calling poor souls who banged up the family car in an accident. "Perhaps we can help with your short-term transportation needs."

The Golden Gate

A real estate guerrilla in California hands an extra three dollars toll and a business card to the toll collector as he crosses the bridge from exclusive Marin County into San Francisco. "I'd like to pay for the car behind me as well. Please give him this." Nine out of ten times, the other driver calls, at least to say "Thank you." He's sold several expensive homes as a result, and at 6 percent commission, he can afford to drive back and forth across the bridge all day, positioning himself in front of BMWs, Cadillacs, and Mercedes Benzes.

Going up?

A life insurance agent in Arizona carries a pocketful of business cards, and when he boards a crowded elevator, he faces the group and, as he hands out his cards, asks, "I guess you're wondering why I called this meeting? Like this elevator, the price of everything is going up, and there's a good chance that your house is currently underinsured. I'd like to offer you all a free review." The doors open, and he makes his exit.

Fashion show

In Phoenix, an alluring young woman saunters through the hotel restaurant at the lunch rush, modeling dresses and handing out coupons for a 20 percent discount, each rolled into a scroll and tied with a bit of colored ribbon. "My store is just across the street," she says, "and this jump suit I'm wearing is only seventy-nine dollars." *Lovely.* Ten minutes later she's back, wearing something different. The customers love it. So does the restaurant owner, whose sales are up as a result of the fashion shows.

Extra lettuce

In Fort Collins, Colorado, a sub sandwich shop owner tucks a twenty-dollar bill, wrapped in Saran, into every one-hundredth sub they make. They've built a loyal base of university students who are hoping to hit the jackpot, and at lunch, people jockey for position in line, hoping to be the next lucky customer.

Touchdown

A cellular-telephone guerrilla in Dallas takes two hundred business cards to every Cowboys home game and tosses them into the air by handfuls whenever they score. About a dozen fans will pick up one of the cards and call. It works so well, she's now seen at many Dallas Maverick basketball games as well.

Photo op

Denise wanted to expand her accounting practice, so she bought a two-by-three-inch ad in the small-town newspaper. She arranged in advance for the printer to leave the ad blank except for a line across the bottom inviting readers to file her business card for future reference. As the papers came off the press, she and her husband stuck her colorful photo business cards into the blank space with double-stick tape. Months later she was still hearing from readers.

Stamps

Always use real stamps. Your materials are much more likely to get through to your intended party than metered mail. Real guerrillas use several stamps of smaller denominations. When appropriate, write on the envelope, in longhand: "Here's the information you requested."

First class

A new assistant in the Denver office of a consulting firm was instructed to include a business card in every piece of outgoing mail. The boss said, "If it has first-class postage on it, include a card." When the accountant gave her a handful of bills to mail out, she followed the rule to the letter. A call came in: "This is the Personnel Department at Public Service Company [the electric utility], and our people down in billing gave us your card. Exactly what kind of training do you do?" The contact resulted in a contract worth thousands of dollars.

All aboard

A tax accountant who commutes from Concord regularly walks the length of the BART train waiting to see a friendly smile from a well-dressed businessperson before he'll sit down. He's found that when he does, a conversation will ensue and he'll be asked what he does. His brother guerrilla in Chicago uses the same "eye contact" approach on the "L" trains there, and he recently reported it also works in stadiums just before a big game.

A senior partner in an Atlanta advertising agency insists on flying first class because of the class of prospects he meets on airplanes. The difference in fares has been more than justified by several big-dollar clients he's met on transcontinental flights.

The screwdriver call

A cash register guerrilla who works a route in the Midwest walks into a mom-and-pop store carrying a leather attaché case. "Hi. I'm from (company) and they sent me by to service your cash register."

"I didn't call for a repairman," says the owner.

"Oh, just routine maintenance, and it's a *free* service. Now if you'll just take out the cash drawer, I can get to work." He snaps open his tool-case and pulls out a screwdriver and a paintbrush, removes the cover, clears the tape-path, lubes keys and gears, and strikes up a conversation.

"How long have you had this machine? Have you had any problems with it? Does it always balance your cash? Does it print all the reports you need? Would you like to track sales by department, or by salesperson? How would you like to know how many customers you had each hour of the day, so you could adjust your staffing?" By the time he has the old machine put back together, he's sold the proprietor a new one.

No obligation

A guerrilla out in Honolulu was the company's top TV salesperson. The company's marketing manager decided to drop in and find out what was going on. When he got to the shop he was greeted warmly. "Are you interested in one of our new color stereo sets?"

"Yes, I could be. How much are they?"

"First, you need to tell me where you live on the island. You see, in some locales, for various reasons, the reception is terrible."

Fumbling, the manager responded, "Huh, er, Waikiki."

"Waikiki is the worst for reception. It's hard to predict. What we're going to have to do, then, is have you take one home and try it for a few days and see how it works. No obligation, of course." Of course, the new set works just fine in Waikiki, and isn't likely to be returned, but the "no obligation" trial relieves the prospect's anxiety about getting stuck with poor reception.

Loaner set

A TV dealer in Seattle offers free pickup and delivery with repair service, and a *free loaner set*: a thirty-inch big-screen! ("Sorry it's so big, ma'am, but it's all we have left.") Problem is, the average repair takes about two weeks. No one seems to mind. The family gets spoiled, and three out of four customers eventually take advantage of the generous trade-in offer.

Magic carpet

Every fall, a young entrepreneur in Wyoming buys up carpet remnants by the truckload. He takes out an eight-dollar classified ad in the University of Wyoming newspaper, offering carpets precut to fit the campus-wide ten-by-twelve-foot dorm room. Average markup: 500 percent. In the spring, he buys them back, for a buck each, and hauls them away, saving the University Housing Department a bundle and making a handsome profit for himself. Fresh prospects each semester.

Hot tracks

Campus Audio, also run by a student entrepreneur, sells $100,000 a year in stereo components out of a two-bedroom apartment. He gets promotional albums from a record distributor and offers them free to anyone one wants to come over and listen to some music.

Accelerated computer

Offering free classes on word processing, spreadsheets, and desktop publishing has been the key to the growth of this Denver chain of retail computer stores. A basement classroom is equipped with a big-screen projection monitor, and the walls are lined with workstations. Free introductory seminars are hands-on. Three, sometimes four classes a day, seven days a week, twenty or thirty people at a time, it's a real traffic-builder. Within the first two hours, computer novices have created a printed document that they can put up on the refrigerator.

"People wouldn't bother to come in unless they had at least some interest in computers," the owner says, "but a lot of them are afraid of the technology. By making the classes easy and entertaining, we kindle that ember of interest into a burning desire to buy. The rest is easy."

Big sale

Three adjacent furniture stores compete for traffic in a Cleveland strip mall. The store on the south end put up a huge sign: CLEARANCE SALE, EVERYTHING MUST GO. The store on the north end put up an even bigger sign that read, GREAT SAVINGS, 50% OFF. The guerrilla in the middle hung a small banner over his door that said only, MAIN ENTRANCE.

Parallel lines

A life insurance guerrilla was striking out trying to sell life insurance to students, so she decided to switch to casualty lines instead. She would call on apartment dwellers, explaining that if there were a fire or other disaster, their furniture and contents would not be covered by the landlord's policy. She suggested low-cost renter's insurance. Although the commissions were very small, it was a quick and easy sale. Once she had established herself as *their insurance agent*, the nature of the relationship changed, and she found her casualty customers frequently asking her about life insurance. By using the casualty lines to open the door and build a clientele, she became a top life insurance producer as well.[1]

Getting appointments

Now that you have a name, address, and phone number, you have to make an initial contact.

Your mission

A guerrilla gets appointments by assuming cooperation and demonstrating mutual concern. The mission is to help, assist, support, and empower clients and customers. In getting appointments, a guerrilla is more concerned with being human than in presenting a polished, professional image. The guerrilla establishes the human bond before trying to create a business bond.

Listen to how one guerrilla we heard of gets an appointment:

"Mr. Prospect, I'm not really sure why my boss asked me to call. Does your firm ever buy electronic components?"

"Sure. Our main business is servicing refrigeration equipment, but we also build our own line of controls."

"That's very interesting, sounds like we ought to get together. Do you have your calendar handy?"

"Yes, it's right here . . ."

"What day are you looking at?"

"I'm looking at today."

---

[1] Many classic prospecting stories originated with the "World's Greatest Salesman," Joe Girard.

"Uh-oh, I can't make it today. How about Thursday, or would Friday be better?"

"Friday, I suppose."

"Okay, and since I picked the day, you pick the time."

You may want to copy these phrases on a three-by-five card and keep it with you until you become comfortable using them.

Turning a cold call into a referred lead

When beginning your cold calls for the day, proper planning will ensure you have to make only one. At the conclusion of your first call in a particular area, ask, "John, I will be visiting other people in this area. If you were me, who would you call on next?" Wait for John's response.

When your prospect suggests a name, ask, "Why did you pick him?" Make that individual your next call and use the introduction from the first cold call as a referral. This sounds like, "Harry, I was visiting with John Jones of the ABC Company earlier this morning, and when I asked John who else he thought I should show my product to, he suggested you. Let me ask, why do you think he picked you?" Your new prospect will give you a warm reception and qualify himself in seconds.

The power of guerrilla prospecting

Gathering current, accurate information about your market, then using it in unconventional ways to create an advantage, that's the power of guerrilla prospecting. Centers of influence are great sources of information, but the best sources are the prospects themselves, their environment, and their behavior. The guerrilla reads the signs that lead to the sale.

The more information you have about the position and movements of your marketplace, the better your chances are for finding prospects, making the right approach, and getting appointments. *Information* is your most powerful weapon, and *surprise* is your most lethal tactic. In every industry we've analyzed, the top producers are not necessarily the best presenters or the strongest closers. They're the best prospectors.

3
The Mind Map

Why do prospects act the way they do?

Guerrillas in the nineties know a great deal about how the human brain operates. This knowledge gives them a real edge in dealing with prospects.

We've done some homework to help you understand how your prospects think, how they will react to you, and how they will make decisions. We've outlined *seven clearly identifiable personality types*, or phases, and carefully analyzed the three that you'll encounter most frequently. We call this summary the *Mind Map*, and it's one of the most advanced weapons in the guerrilla's arsenal.

Most of us adopt one of these phases as our *primary* personality type, but we may *shift* from one phase to another, depending on the relationship, the circumstances, or stress. Whenever people interact, they *invariably* do so from one of these phases.

Let's look at an example. A senior insurance salesman, and a guerrilla at heart, was introducing a new voluntary retirement plan to employees of a northern California county, but he couldn't seem to stir up much interest. The plan was good, and this sales agent had worked long and hard to get it approved by the county government.

During the enrollment period, he sat in a small room in the county office waiting for employees to come by to hear about the new plan and sign up for it. In the first week, only five people came to hear the good news.

The first employee was so shy she hardly said a word. She sat with ankles crossed, hands folded in her lap, and listened quietly to the presentation. She didn't ask a single question or even offer her name, let alone sign up. She seemed afraid of meeting any stranger. "My boss just asked me to come over and pick up some literature," she said as she left.

The next was aggressive, arrogant, and evasive. She asked pointed questions about dividends and rates of return, then stared out the window as he answered. She expressed concern at "being sold a bill of goods," but she was certain she knew how to deal with salespeople. "'I'd look like a fool,'" she said, "if I jumped into something like this without reviewing it thoroughly." She took the prospectus and left.

A third employee was very polite and seemed to take a sincere interest, nodding his head in agreement with everything. He was a perfect gentleman, agreeing that it was a fine plan, and that he had a real need. He even showed the guerrilla pictures of his children, and talked about his hopes for the future. He was very apologetic in the end, but he didn't sign up. From his objections and questions, it was obvious that he really hadn't heard half the presentation.

The fourth was direct and distant, as if the only reason he was there was that he'd been told to go. He wanted cold facts and figures, not the warm picture of a comfortable retirement he was hearing. "How do I know that this is the best plan available? What guarantee do I have that your company will achieve this rate of return?" he asked. He challenged the company's reputation and the salesperson's credibility.

The fifth employee was delightful. She seemed confident, relaxed, and genuine. She asked relevant questions, listened attentively, and, to her ultimate benefit, she signed up. As she was filling out the forms, the guerrilla wondered what made this person so different.

He asked other employees about her. Everyone who worked with her commented on how good they feel when she's around. She's always fair, they said, and she cares about people and their work, and she shows it. She's always willing to do her share, and more. The guerrilla was beginning to understand. With her philosophy, he could see why she was able to recognize the benefits of the new plan without feeling anxious about the salesperson's reaction.

He decided to follow her example. If I were really committed to being *fair, caring,* and *sharing,* he wondered, what would be the fairest way to get this information to all the county employees, to show them that we care about their quality of life at retirement?

That gave him an idea. It would be unfair, and perhaps even unlawful, if all the employees were not given an equal opportunity to learn about the plan and a chance to accept or reject it. He raised this question with the county counsel. The counsel agreed, and issued a memo to all county employees.

To be fair, everyone would be required to attend a group meeting in an auditorium where they could hear the whole presentation and ask questions. After the meeting they could either enroll in the new plan or sign a waiver saying that they had heard a complete explanation and decided to decline.

With this new strategy, over 80 percent of eligible employees enrolled in two weeks. The salesman repeated the tactic in other cities and counties all over the state. His fair-for-all-concerned approach increased sales dramatically, rocketing him to top producer in his company.

By observing one of the principles by which guerrillas operate, this salesman was able to find an unorthodox way to deliver his message to a large number of prospects, and discovered greater *personal* and *financial* success. He started to wonder if there was a way to be more effective with prospects like the first four he had met.

A matter of principle

Have you ever wondered why some people seem to be so much more effective on the job? Or why some people are more successful in their careers and more fulfilled in their personal lives? The difference lies in a few fundamental principles that empower them to be more effective and realize more of their potential. Like the fifth county employee, some people seem to have discovered these secrets.

They are the 20 percent of any sales force who produce 80 percent of the business. They're the ones who are well thought of and have satisfying relationships. They're the ones who perform at the highest levels and get the bonuses and the promotions.

Leading sales performers have two universal characteristics in common: they operate out of high levels of personal maturity, and they strive to unlock the potential of their prospects. They *work to control and direct their own thoughts*, and they *work to understand the thinking of their client*.

Success in sales does not depend on technical skills. Every day we buy sophisticated technology from people who know less about it than we do. It does not depend on hard work; we've seen many hardworking failures. It does not depend on native intelligence. Unfulfilled genius is a cliché. But there's a vast reservoir of potential waiting to be unleashed in our personal and professional lives.

The greatest frontier of the Information Age is the human mind. It's difficult to scan a magazine rack or watch a weekend of TV without encountering some new information on how we think. New findings are released daily.

The Mind Map

We have summarized these findings into a model of behavior and personality we call the *Mind Map*. It's a graphic representation that divides mind function into seven personalities which, because we shift from one to another, we call phases.

This model is called the Mind Map because it's a blueprint of the seven personality phases. Using its insights is like putting your hands directly on the control lever of your mind. It provides a powerful explanation of the personalities you'll encounter and how they relate to each other. This map is used by guerrillas to *quickly identify the personality phase of their prospects*, clients, and customers. In the following chapters we'll be giving you specific strategies to use with people operating in each of these phases.

The Mind Map is based on the works of Swiss philosopher Jean Piaget, the American sociologist Abraham Maslow, Nobel laureate Roger Sperry, Harvard professor Lawrence Kohlberg, and psychologists Alan Schoonmaker, Vernon Woolf, and Vern Black, so it reflects the most current research in psychology and behavioral science. It's been adapted from the clinical environment for business applications and has been validated in hundreds of seminars and workshops we've conducted all over the world.

It is, nevertheless, just a model, and like any good model, it's an oversimplification. Like a pair of binoculars, a model allows you to examine things close-up, but it also distorts your perspective and cuts off your peripheral vision. People are complex beings, and it's unrealistic to expect to dissect the total psyche in one book. That is not our intent.

Modeling is a useful way to approach any complex problem. Like a chart or a mission plan, the Mind Map is intended to help you navigate the unfamiliar territory of personality in the hundreds of new prospects that you meet.

Perhaps you've heard parents comment, "Oh, it's just a *phase* the kid's going through." Over the course of a lifetime, we normally experience all seven phases.

When you understand this Mind Map, you will immediately begin to decode the behavior of prospects and clients. As your comprehension increases, so does your selling skill. *People at different phases have unique needs, wants, and expectations.* By observing simple patterns in their behavior, you can anticipate the questions they'll ask, the objections they'll raise, and even the type of information they need in order to buy. You'll deliver your selling ordinance with surgical precision.

Guerrillas are flexible

By moving from one phase to another at will, you'll have the capacity to deal effectively with anyone, under nearly any circumstance. You will begin to see where personality conflicts are created, and improve the atmosphere of these relationships. You can quickly move to a different phase, gaining the psychological high ground that produces greater results. You'll exhibit confidence and inspire it in others. As a result, you'll have relationships based on mutual trust, shared concerns, and open communication.

The Amoral Phase

We all begin life as infants, and because the behavior of infants is neither moral nor immoral, we call this the *Amoral* phase. In this phase, the mind is preoccupied with processes that are *physical* and *reactive* in nature, without consideration of ethics or morals, good or bad. During the Amoral phase, infants have little awareness of reality beyond their own bodies and their immediate surroundings. They are totally unacquainted with the needs of others. This is normal for very young children. It is not so normal in adults. You will, however, occasionally meet a prospect who is operating in the Amoral phase.

The general characteristics of the *Amoral* phase are *eating, sleeping, crying,* and mentally *going away,* passively watching the world go by. The dominant needs are *physical.* Alternately, they will withdraw and shut down to recuperate from the stresses of a world to which they are not yet fully adapted.

Over a period of time, if a child experiences parents who are themselves Amoral, that is, rough, brutal, or abusive, the child may adopt the Amoral phase as his primary mode and remain in the Amoral phase throughout life. This child may have difficulty moving to other phases. Feelings of anger, jealousy, insecurity, or fear will dominate.

As adults, we all slip into the Amoral phase temporarily when we need to escape or recover, and a certain amount of that may be healthy.

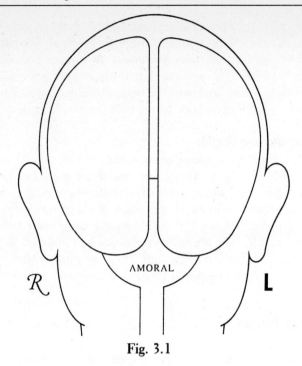

Fig. 3.1

Some may sleep all weekend, others get drunk, and still others watch TV or slip away to a basement hobby shop. Adults who are stuck in the Amoral phase are not functional in society. They represent a small percentage of the general population, but are usually diagnosed as psychopathic or sociopathic.

Guerrillas call this the "Leave Me Alone" phase, and it can be triggered by unusual events or extreme stress. If you encounter a prospect who is temporarily in this phase, gracefully end the conversation and attempt another meeting. It's impossible to have any kind of meaningful discussion with someone who is temporarily shut down.

The Ego Phase

When infants discover that they are individuals, unique and separate from their parents, they normally move out of the Amoral phase and into the *Ego* phase. In it, children perceive themselves as the center of

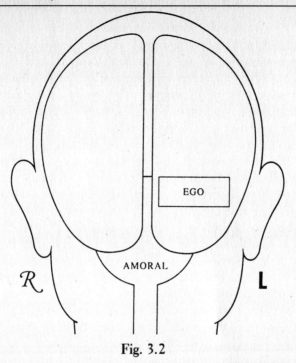

Fig. 3.2

the universe, and all other people are placed in their life to serve them. In normal maturation, this phase develops around age two.

The general characteristics of the *Ego* phase are *possessiveness, attention seeking*, and a need for *control*. There's a preoccupation with one's own needs and wants, without consideration for the needs of others.

Kids often get their Ego phase needs met by throwing a temper tantrum. Parents call this phase "the Terrible Twos." It's during this phase that kids develop language and, with it, the capacity to ask for what they want. They are also learning to assert themselves and set limits, and learning how much they can get away with. They learn two very important words, which they use frequently: "mine" and "no!"

The dominant needs of the Ego phase are *material:* my toys, my book, and my mommy! They will push things to the limit just to see what will happen. They can be loud, violent, even maliciously destructive.

A healthy Ego is essential for all functional adults. It's what motivates us to strive to have a better life. Ego is the resource state from which we challenge convention and develop new ways of doing things that defy the old patterns.

Children who are chronically spoiled by their parents may adopt the Ego phase as their primary mode of adult behavior. Their dishonesty takes the form of self-aggrandizement. In their quest to gain the attention and recognition they valued as a child, they stretch the truth about themselves. As adults, they're often perceived as demanding, self-centered, and egocentric. There's a simple reason for this perception; it's because they *are*. They are often overly critical, knocking everything and everyone, which, of course, are never as good as they are.

All of us know adults who are stuck in this phase. In fact, psychologists tell us that 30 to 40 percent of the population operates primarily out of Ego. They're preoccupied with themselves, *their* things, *their* ideas, *their* accomplishments. They're very status conscious: *my* house, *my* boat, *my* sports car, or territory conscious: *my* corner office. "If you take a pencil out of my desk again, I'll break your thumbs!" They "break up, just to make up," going through endless cycles of conflict and resolution, and may not realize that there can be very severe consequences for this behavior.

Excessive Ego behavior is socially unhealthy. Like the screaming toddler in the aisle of the grocery store, these people get their way by throwing a fit, making others uncomfortable with the intensity, and eventually getting them to cave in. There's a part deep inside all of us that just wants to smack 'em on the fanny and send them to bed without supper. Unfortunately, if your prospect happens to be operating in the Ego phase, this is not a good option.

Here the mind creates all the self-serving "gimme, gimme, gimmes." In Western society we exploit this mental phase; much of our marketing is based on it. In fact, the Ego-phase, "You deserve a break today" marketing mentality is a multibillion-dollar American industry. This phase is best known to guerrillas as the "Do it *my* way *now*" phase.

Your best approach with Ego prospects is to demonstrate your leadership, and don't hold back. They want to know if you're good enough for them to bother with. Be smooth and positive. Let them know that you're the best and that you represent only the best.

The Pleaser Phase

At some point early in life, the mind learns that not only is it a separate ego, but that *there are other egos* in the world as well. Survival appears to depend on pleasing others.

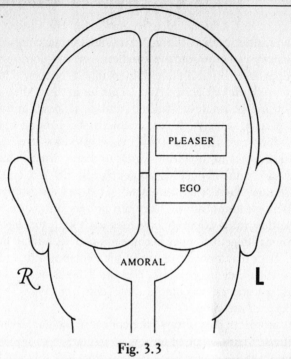

Fig. 3.3

The mind begins to maneuver to get along with other people. This third developmental level is called the *Pleaser* phase because the most common characteristic of this phase is the desire to please others in order to survive.

The general characteristics of the *Pleaser* phase are *compliance*, *helpfulness*, and *generosity*. Children at this phase say, "I love you, Mommy," about a dozen times a day. They may give a favorite toy to a playmate or volunteer to wash the dishes. This "I'll-please-you-if-you-please-me" mode usually begins in children around age seven or eight.

Developmentally, the child is learning the important social skills of cooperation and mutuality. There is a basic understanding of the concepts of sharing and teamwork, and a sensitivity to the needs and feelings of others.

The dominant needs are *psychological*. They are motivated by acceptance and approval. These needs are met through doing unsolicited favors, or if they've fallen into disfavor, by being overly solicitous and apologetic.

As adults, a healthy Pleaser mode helps us create and build relationships. It helps us to give recognition and approval to others when it's deserved. But it has an addictive dark side. The Pleaser phase may be used to control others through manipulation or emotional blackmail. This mode can grow into the mindless, you-can-do-no-wrong euphoria of puppy love. But it is difficult to maintain, because it leaves the more basic needs of the Ego and Amoral phases unmet. After operating from the Pleaser phase for a while, the mind notices that this relationship isn't pleasing *enough*. It may mentally slip back to Ego, throwing a "you-don't-care-about-me-a-bit" fit, or withdraw into Amoral.

Adults stuck in the Pleaser phase as their primary mode of behavior may have difficulty setting appropriate limits and boundaries. They don't know when or how to say no. They may be syrupy and insincere in their communication. They can be very difficult to work with because they make commitments they can't keep, or they avoid making decisions altogether. They become yes-people, but fail to deliver in the end. They may respond to unrealistic demands with a sound "can do" even when they haven't got a chance. They may overdo simple tasks, creating unnecessary complication, costs, or delay. Dishonesty takes the form of omission.

As prospects, they always offer coffee. In their anxiety to please, they subjugate their own point of view, so it's hard to know where they really stand.

Some 30 percent of the adult population operates primarily out of the Pleaser personality. This also has been the stereotypically accepted role for women in our culture: the loyal secretary, the meticulous housewife, or the devoted mother.

Your best approach with Pleasers is to be friendly, take a real interest in them, and be somewhat assertive, since Pleasers tend to put off making decisions.

The Authority Phase

Some time in the teen years we realize that not only are we separate egos, and that there are other egos, but that there are whole *systems* or groups of egos we belong to. As we grow, the mind tires of trying endlessly to please others or trying to fulfill the images others have of us. The maturing mind now seeks the right way. As the mind becomes dissatisfied with Amoral, Ego, and Pleaser behavior, it shifts to the *Authority* phase.

The general characteristic of the *Authority* phase is the need for

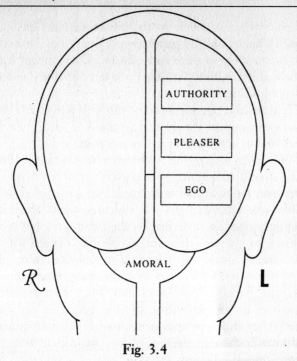

Fig. 3.4

rules. A person in this phase looks to laws, books, experts, and authority figures to show it the *right* way to behave. This mind says, "I will learn how to get along, how to become a good employee, a good supervisor, a good husband or wife. I'll learn the right rules and do my duty." The mind may become overly *judgmental*, reliant on the "one and only" right way when there may be many right ways.

During the Authority phase, we define our identities by applying labels. "I am: male/female, white/black, Catholic/Protestant/Jewish, Italian/Armenian, smart/dumb, talented/athletic," or not.

The dominant needs of the Authority phase are *social*, so we develop networks of people who fit our labels, who are like us. By the time we were freshmen in high school, we knew *exactly* who we could have lunch with, who we could sit next to on the bus, who we could invite to the Saturday dance, and we didn't *dare* violate those boundaries. Unfortunately, this phase is also the source of the stereotyping we develop about other groups. The "us versus them" mentality begins here, together with other forms of prejudice. Anyone who doesn't fit our model of what's *right* (meaning like us) is *wrong* and is judged to be inferior and undesirable.

Authority-phase people are the rule-makers in society, and represent about 10 percent of the population. They're the doctors and the lawyers, the captains of ships and industry. They are our leaders, our experts, and our authorities. They are our "how-to" writers and "show biz" personalities.

They are also our tastemakers, our cult gurus, and our radio-talk-show sex therapists. We depend on them to tell us how to dress, how to eat, and in general, how to live our lives.

The healthy side of the Authority phase is that it allows us to live within structured systems, such as everyone in North America agreeing to drive on the right side of the road. Authority behavior becomes unhealthy when thinking gets inflexible and rigid. There is nothing inherently correct about driving on the right or the left side of the road; it's just a handy rule. However, people who operate with Authority as their primary mode are bound up by policies, rules, and structure. There is only *one* correct way to do anything. In extreme cases, they're moralistic, dictatorial, and intolerant. They often become the arrogant know-it-all or the pessimistic wet blanket who's certain "it can't be done." They also show up as perfectionists. They are generally too rigid to deal with the complexities of life, for which there can never be enough rules. Dishonesty takes the form of appeal to higher authority.

It's been suggested that we take teenagers right out of high school and put them into the White House, the Congress, and the Pentagon while they still really *do* know *everything*.

Authority-phase people are not satisfied for very long because they've relinquished responsibility for their actions and relationships, turning them over to the "experts." Because of this, many Authority minds invent strategies that endlessly move them in and out of the other phases.

Guerrillas refer to these folks as "Your Honor" or "His Lordship." Your best approach with Authority prospects is to avoid friendly gestures and stick to the facts. Appeal to systems, logic, and quoted sources.

The Principle Phase

Around thirtysomething, usually after having been involved in a stable personal relationship, we may start to recognize that there are cer-

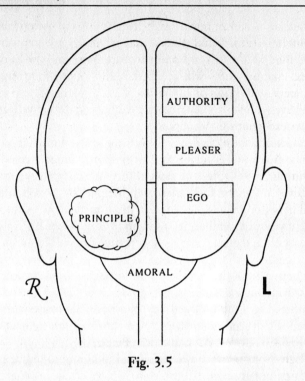

Fig. 3.5

tain fundamentals that make life work, something more basic than rules. By now we've created something enduring, something in cooperation with others: we've borne children, built a house, or started a business. A recognition dawns that these things are made possible by underlying universal principles. This is the beginning of the fifth phase, the *Principle* phase. This is where guerrillas originate.

The general characteristics of the *Principle* phase can be summed up in three words: *fair*, *care*, and *share*. This phase begins with the development of an *acceptance* of how people are, exactly as they are, and exactly as they are not. Differences are celebrated rather than condemned, and there is a *suspension of the judgment* characteristic of the Authority phase. A corresponding *acceptance of self* develops as well, neither subjugated, as in Pleasers, nor elevated, as in Egos.

Your ability to maintain the *Principle* phase depends on your ability to be fair, to communicate your caring, and to do a little more than your share.

It takes a concentrated effort to develop a sense of fairness, a real caring for yourself and others, and an ability to consistently do your fair share of any task at hand. Because there are always exceptions to rules, mature adults will get their needs met by following principles, not the specific laws of Authority-phase thinking. These principles are intuitively obvious; they need no outside confirmation, and there are never exceptions to principles.

As illustrated in figure 3.5, moving to the Principle phase is a big jump. It requires a major shift in thinking. Once a mind can understand systems of rules and laws at the Authority phase, it can begin to discern the more fundamental principles by which life functions. You'll notice that Principle isn't positioned *above* Authority, as you might presume. Rather, it's a *lateral shift* in perspective, away from the step-by-step, logical mind to the creative mind. The jump to the Principle phase is a quantum leap. It's a move from the *objective* to the *subjective*, from the *rational* to the *intuitive*, from the left brain to the right brain. It is a barrier most minds never permanently cross.

Instead of a rigid, closed box, the Principle phase is illustrated as a cloud with vague boundaries. The nature of the right brain phases is more open and less definable than that of the left brain.

Transitions between the individual phases of the right brain are not distinct, but gradual. All three are aspects of one another and are collectively referred to as the *Principled phases*.

As with most of life, once a barrier is overcome, a great gift awaits. The amazing thing is after you move into the Principle phase, your memory, concentration, creativity, and intuition all begin to increase dramatically. Even your interpersonal relationships improve, and you become a much more productive, creative salesperson, a guerrilla salesperson. More on this in chapter 4, "The Guerrilla Mind."

The principled mind begins to experience that there are no real problems, only opportunities. You are able to control yourself and influence others. You are now more easily able to tap your creative self for better, more powerful selling. Your general health improves, and life takes on a positive and beautiful growth. At the Principle phase, you are on the road to becoming you at your highest potential.

All it takes is following a life of being *fair* to all concerned, really *caring* about the people in your life, and being really willing to do your *share* of whatever tasks come your way. Consistently practice these three principles for a month or so and you'll begin to notice a real difference in how others relate to you.

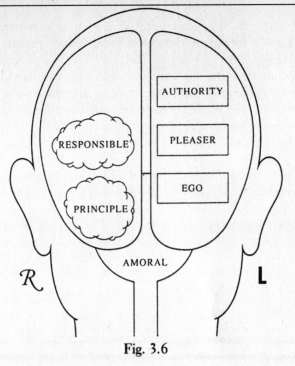

Fig. 3.6

The Responsible Phase

At some point, usually later in life, we finally recognize the inescap-
able truth of cause and effect: that *everything* that we've ever done,
everything that we know, everything that we have are the direct consequences of the choices we've made during our lifetime. The mind
that is able to *apply principles on a responsible basis* enters the *Responsible* phase.

The *Responsible* phase is achieved by those who view themselves as
the *cause* and *source* of *everything* in their lives. This is not simply an
intellectual belief about what it means to be a responsible parent or a
responsible citizen. It's a profound acceptance that "This is it, and I'm
responsible for how it turns out. This is my life. This is the body it's
housed in. This is my family. This is my profession. This is my planet.
I'm in charge of my own life."

The general characteristic of the *Responsible* phase is in its name:
responsibility. At this phase we accept accountability for our actions

and outcomes. Who we are and what we achieve are no longer attributed to conditions of birth, bad luck, or our parents' strengths or weaknesses.

It is the sense that I am my brother's keeper. Not that I'm responsible for creating his pain, but that I can, in my awareness of it, ease that pain. It is at this phase that we fully understand about *sharing*. Do you recall being told as a child that we always leave the picnic area a little cleaner than we found it? This is doing your share of the task at hand and a bit more.

George Bernard Shaw summed up the Responsible phase in the following statement taken in part from the Epistle Dedicatory to *Man and Superman*:

This is the true joy in life; the being used for a purpose, recognized by yourself as a mighty one; the being a force of Nature instead of a feverish, selfish little clod of ailments and grievances, complaining that the world will not devote itself to making you happy.

I am of the opinion that my life belongs to the whole community and as long as I live it is my privilege to do for it whatever I can. I want to be thoroughly used up when I die, for the harder I work, the more I live.

I rejoice in life for its own sake. Life is no 'brief candle' to me. It is a sort of splendid torch which I have got a hold of for the moment, and I want to make it burn as brightly as possible before handing it on to future generations.

The Universal Phase

This is the phase of those who have mastered life and represents the *Universal* mind. Nearly everyone has experienced this phase at least once; however, staying there would be exceptional. *This is you at your highest potential.* At this phase, people fully integrate the logical and creative minds, integrate themselves with others, and integrate the mental, physical, and spiritual realms of their experiences.

The *Universal* phase is expressed by those who *consistently live by correct principles*. They find peace and success in every aspect of life, both the positive and the apparently negative.

The general characteristics of the *Universal* phase are *freedom, empowerment*, and *ecstasy*. This person maximizes freedom for everyone by living and teaching correct principles, then allowing others to govern their own lives and handle their own responsibilities.

Empowerment requires having direction and goals. *Purpose* is a pre-

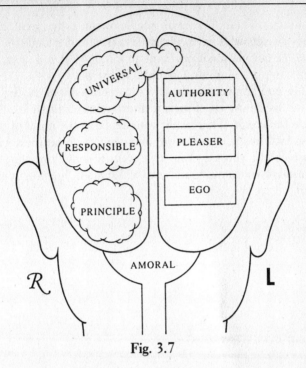

Fig. 3.7

requisite. As the world has become more and more industrialized, many of us have lost track of our purpose in life. For many, the purpose of their jobs is unclear, and how their jobs relate to the purpose of the company is not apparent. People act powerfully when they know and understand the contribution they can make.

Universal-phase people find ecstasy in every aspect of life. This does not mean some kind of mindless euphoria or superpositive mental attitude. Ecstasy means fun, not frivolousness or idle amusement, but rather fun in the recreational sense, as in *re*-creation. Work is more than fun for these people; it's recreational.

In the Universal phase, there is a connection between the spiritual and temporal aspects of life. Body, mind, and spirit work together in harmony. You embrace and accept change as the inevitable consequence of growth.

There are Universal-phase individuals among us. They're found in our churches and in our synagogues; they are also found in our businesses, factories, and schools. We often don't hear of them, but we feel the difference their maturity makes. Many of them stand out in history, not as celebrities but as catalytic figures who made superhuman contributions. These Universal people include the great teachers and moral leaders who have guided us to new understandings. In our own time, certain personalities come to mind: Mother Teresa, Martin Luther King, Jr., Einstein, Gandhi, Gorbachev.

The guerrilla constantly strives to operate out of the highest possible phase. By basing all of their relationships on principles, they demonstrate *leadership*. This instills confidence in the mind of the prospect. They will like you, trust you, and want to do business with you, because of who you are. Your *true identity* shows through, not your affiliation or your image, and they will stand in line to buy from you.

The Mind Map

The Inner Mind: The Primitive Reactionary Mind

The **Amoral Phase** of infants and certain adults who act without any morality; those who simply shut down and go away when things get rough. **Best Approach: reschedule and exit.**

The Left Mind: The Logical Linear Mind

The **Ego Phase** of children and many adults who see themselves as the center of the universe; self-centered adults who are in endless cycles of fighting and making up. **Best Approach: smooth and positive.**

The **Pleaser Phase** of youngsters and adults who survive by being nice and doing good. This maturity allows Pleasers to manipulate others to get their needs met. **Best Approach: interested and assertive.**

The **Authority Phase** of young adults and others who come to expect rules and agreements to govern their lives. They become excessively duty bound in their urge to do things the right way. **Best Approach: facts and logic.**

The Right Mind: The Creative Intuitive Mind

The **Principle Phase** of mature adults who know that their life works to the extent that they follow principles such as being fair with everyone, really caring for others, and doing more than a fair share of the task at hand. **Best Approach: show you're fair-care-share.**

The **Responsible Phase** of mature adults who know that they are the cause and the source of everything that comes into their lives. They take full responsibility for the situations in which they find themselves. **Best Approach: stress community/company good.**

The **Universal Phase** of those who constantly reach their highest potential by living a principled life, balancing the right and left brain. This is the phase of one who finds peace and success in every aspect of life. Freedom, empowerment, and ecstasy are the hallmarks. **Best Approach: relax, just tell your story.**

4
The Guerrilla Mind

Sell is a four-letter word

Suggest sales as a career to most college sophomores and you'll raise suspicious laughter. They'd rather pursue something more "professional," like medicine, law, accounting, or management. The truth is that many salespeople earn *more* than doctors or lawyers, and the majority of *Fortune* 500 presidents started their careers in sales. It's the fast track to professional leadership, income, and prestige, because people who can generate business are the lifeblood of any organization. They're in constant demand. As it turns out, sales is one of the most secure careers you can pursue.

Unfortunately, most people view sales as a temporary wayside, like selling magazines in college or clerking in a retail shop until they can get a "real job." Attracted by the income and the freedom, some stay on. They either enjoy working with people or they find the challenge stimulating. A few will eventually achieve substantial success, building their income through a constituency of satisfied repeat customers. Some spend their careers hopping from company to company, following the latest technical fads or economic trends.

Guerrillas are different. They're on a mission. When you ask them about their work, they glow with enthusiasm. We met one who works for a plumbing supply house in Kokomo, Indiana. His job wasn't as glamorous as a stockbroker's or a real estate agent's, but he was genuinely excited about his work.

"You know," he says, "plumbing is the basis of all our modern sanitation. It makes living in cities possible. Without it, we'd be plagued by all sorts of nasties like cholera. I don't think anyone wants to go back to the disease-ridden days of the outdoor privy with its crescent moon on the door."

Now there's a man with a *vision*. He's not just selling pipe and porcelain. He's building a future, making it possible for thousands of people to lead comfortable, healthy lives.

Another works in an appliance store. "My favorite lines are these new audio/video systems that integrate a TV, a VCR, and digitally processed stereo sound. It blows people away when they really hear the decoded soundtrack from a videotape, and it completely *amazes* them when they learn that they can put that same movie-house experience right in their own living room. It brings families together."

These guerrillas aren't just thinking about the commission or the next order. They're driven by a sense of purpose. They're excited by the possibilities of their product, and they're eager to share it with others. Whether it's architecture or advertising, hardware or hydraulic fluid, they believe in their products and the benefits they bring. They protect the interests of their employer and are sensitive to the needs of customers.

If this sounds a lot like the Principle phase, you're right. Guerrillas understand the principles of business, and know that if they're fair to all concerned, really care about the people they deal with, and do their share to present their products, their success will be guaranteed.

Three things all guerrillas have in common:

Operating consistently out of the Principle phase requires a commitment to fundamental values that all guerrillas share.

Integrity

Guerrillas demonstrate *integrity* in all their dealings, giving customers the facts, resisting the temptation to exaggerate benefits or to fabricate small details. They are truly knowledgeable about the competition and research constantly to keep their information current and reliable, staying on the leading edge. They deliver on every promise made to the prospect and protect their employer from undue risks. It's a balancing act, weighing the interests of the customer against the interests of the company. Once the high-wire of your integrity begins to falter, you are doomed to fall.

Initiative

Guerrillas must have the *initiative* to be a self-starter, to set goals, and to manage their own time. They are comfortable approaching strangers, secure in their self-esteem, and anxious to share their products' benefits. They develop contacts everywhere, at church, at the grocery store, at ball games, anywhere they can find people they can help.

Discipline

Guerrillas have the *discipline* to keep going, systematically planning presentations and working their territory, consistently following up on past customers. They are not easily discouraged, because they know there will always be *someone* who needs their product or service. They keep careful records and use the information they gather to generate more business. They have their ups and downs, but their production is consistent because they are systematic.

If this sounds difficult, don't be discouraged. All this actually makes the guerrilla's job easier in the long run. Their integrity makes others *trust* them, their inititive makes others *respect* them, and their discipline makes others *depend* on them. In time, the guerrilla's customers wouldn't consider going anywhere else.

Human nature

Even guerrillas succumb to immature behavior, what we often call "human nature." Guerrillas have an objective: to make sales. But they also share the same cognitive needs as their prospects.

In many jobs, a worker's performance is hard to measure. Employees can relax and work at whatever pace they're most comfortable. But selling performance is immediate and measurable, so you can't afford the luxury of acting in ways that make yourself comfortable at the prospect's expense.

Trying to satisfy your own psychological needs may interfere with making sales. When prospects indicate that they want you to behave in certain ways, you will be more effective *if you respond to their needs rather than your own.*

Guerrillas are sensitive to prospects' priorities

Acceptance

Everyone wants to be accepted. Salespeople risk rejection every time they call, and the fear of rejection is probably their major cause of failure. The simplest way for them to sidestep rejection is to avoid calling on people and avoid asking for a commitment. Less drastically, they can dodge *feeling* rejected by being cold, impersonal, or arrogant. All of these actions reduce their productivity and actually increase their chances of being rejected, by their *employer.*

People are the most receptive when they are physically and psychologically at ease, so guerrillas communicate their concern by striving to control factors that might distract the prospect. They remain focused and relaxed in difficult situations. They avoid pressure tactics, and if the timing of a call is poor, they reschedule. They try to arrange calls, presentations, and delivery at the *customer's* convenience rather than their own. The result is they are accepted, even welcomed, by even the toughest prospects.

Respect

Everyone also wants to be respected, but in selling, your status is clearly lower than your prospects'. You come to them, and they have the right to reject you, to make demands, or to insist that you defer to their schedules.

Many salespeople feel uncomfortable with this difference in status. They may try to build themselves up by boasting or putting the competition down. This frustrates the prospect, and both parties become uncomfortable.

Guerrillas communicate respect for the prospect, the competition, and themselves. Guerrillas are at ease with people of every status, treating the café waitress or the hotel bellman with the same deference they would offer the president of a major company. Their impartiality makes everyone feel important and respected for the contribution they make.

Enjoyment

Naturally, everyone wants to enjoy their work, but pursuing personal interests at the customer's expense can be disastrous. For example, most investors want their stockbrokers to concentrate on achieving financial goals. They want simple, understandable solutions to complex problems. But many brokers find personal financial problems boring. They'd rather talk about technical analysis, econometrics, or the impact of the Federal Reserve Bank on interest rates. These discussions may entertain the broker, but they confuse and irritate most investors.

Guerrillas are interested in their specialty, but they are even *more* interested in *people*. Every account presents a new and stimulating challenge. They ask questions, listen, and learn from their customers, thereby serving them better. They study constantly and pride themselves on their ability to translate abstract technicalities into clear and relevant language.

Relating

Everyone wants to be related to in ways that make them comfortable, but the same actions that make salespeople comfortable may make their prospects very *un*comfortable.

A salesperson who likes to talk, for instance, may frustrate the *prospect's* desire to talk. If the salesperson is more comfortable in an *Ego* role, the prospect may feel inferior and resentful. A salesperson who needs a great deal of warmth from people will alienate *Authority* and *Ego* prospects whose psychological needs are much different.

Guerrillas must, therefore, learn to relate on the prospect's terms, even at the risk of their own discomfort. Guerrillas are like chameleons, adapting to their surroundings, adjusting their pace, their focus, and their approach to suit each individual. Because they are adept at such camouflage, they can move easily among a wide range of personalities. Guerrillas also strive to be authentic. They would never attempt to be something they are not, but rather present the side of their genuine personality that will harmonize with the prospect's. This flexibility empowers them to be highly effective with many different personalities, and for guerrillas who are operating out of the *Principle* phase, it comes naturally.

Types of salespeople

Some years ago, Dr. Alan Schoonmaker first taught that salespeople relate to people in different ways. Some are direct and assertive. Some are warm and friendly. Some are detached and aloof. To illustrate these different sales personalities, we will look at the classic *Ego*-phase, *Pleaser*-phase, *Authority*-phase, and *Principle*-phase personalities outlined in the Mind Map. To demonstrate the potential conflicts, let's look in on the proprietor of a large retail florist as he's being called on by reps from a lighting and electrical supply house. Each is trying to introduce the supply house's new line of energy-saving fluorescent lamps. Remember, the following are caricatures; very few people possess all the characteristics of a phase in the extreme, but you'll be able to clearly see each type.

Ego *salespeople*

Ego salespeople are competitive and high-pressure. They're driven to outsell their comrades, the competition, and even themselves, and are often top producers. But their success is frequently short-lived, subject to the "shooting-star syndrome," because their style does not build the long-term customer loyalty that is so critical in guerrilla selling.

They assume that people don't want to buy and their job is to wear down this resistance with arguments, pressure, and just plain tenacity. Everything is a skirmish for Ego-phase salespeople, and they view the prospect as a pawn in a win/lose game of "let's see who's going to get their way this time."

1. Recon and initial approach

The Ego wants to go where the action is, not sit around gathering information about prospects, so their recon is generally superficial. They prefer dropping in cold to making appointments. They act first and ask questions later, if at all.

Their approach is to fire the first shot in the battle. They try to take control immediately to show the prospect who's boss. They drop names, like, "Mr. Purchasing Agent, I was just across town taking an order from another firm you may have heard of. I can't mention them by name, but their initials are IBM."

Their diagnosis is shallow or nonexistent. Egos assume that they know what prospects need. This Ego-level lighting salesman starts his pitch with "Everyone's interested in saving money, wouldn't you agree? And [without stopping] this new line of watt-saver lamps is going to save you a bundle in electricity."

2. Sales presentations

Egos' presentations are usually well organized and hard-hitting. But since their assessment is poor, the impact may land off-target. "For each four-lamp fixture, you'll save an average of thirty-eight cents a month, and I counted eighty fixtures in your showroom. Only a *fool* would ignore that kind of waste." Great, Mr. Ego. You've just told your prospect he's a fool.

3. Handling objections and closing

The ego-phase salesperson rarely analyzes objections and often gives long, argumentative responses to them. Instead of clarifying the prospect's concerns, the Ego will try to overwhelm the prospect with facts, arguments, and personal pressure.

"But we're trying to create a warm atmosphere in our showroom," objects the prospect, "and we've experimented with a combination of fluorescent and incandescent lighting until we finally feel we have the right color balance."

"And it's wasting a lot of energy!" says the Ego. "I figured you'll save over twelve hundred dollars a year by switching to these watt-saver lamps," he adds, reiterating the planned presentation's key benefit.

Getting the order is the Ego's greatest strength, the ultimate victory, and *not* getting it is the ultimate defeat. So the Ego asks for the order again and again, often putting words in the prospect's mouth, like "don't you," "I figured," "couldn't you" and "wouldn't you agree?"

4. After-sale tracking

For the Ego, following up, what we call tracking, is rare and superficial. Once they have won, they want to move on to the next battle. There's little interest in a long-term relationship. Order in hand, they've claimed their prize and head off for other conquests.

Despite these shortcomings, some Ego-phase salespeople have been extraordinarily successful. Their intense need to win and their drive to influence people may compensate for many of their faults. People sometimes buy just to get them off their backs. They can be effective in a selling battlefield where there are unlimited prospects and limited competition. But this kind of selling is very costly; *it costs five times as much to create a new customer as it does to keep an existing customer.*[1] Egos are most effective selling simple products that require little analysis or user support.

Pleaser *salespeople*

Most people would rather buy from someone who seems to care about them, but excessive acquiescence can be a severe liability. You risk rejection every time you make a sales call or ask for an order, and Pleaser-phase people simply can't afford that risk. Consequently, they don't make a lot of calls, or they call only on people who will receive them warmly. They're amiable and friendly, but they may treat their calls as social occasions rather than as genuine attempts to get business. They assume prospects give business to people they like, and have an

[1] Karl Albrecht and Ron Zemke, *Service America!* (Homewood, Ill.: Dow Jones-Irwin, 1985).

intense need to be liked, but their prospects often refer to them contemptuously as "professional visitors."

1. Recon and initial approach

Pleasers focus on the person, not the business opportunity. They concentrate on learning how to establish the best possible relationship and may gloss over an objective analysis of the prospect's needs. "I was in the neighborhood and thought I'd stop by to see if there's anything I could do for you today."

Their approach is homey, affable, and much too long. They enjoy pleasant conversation and suspect that getting down to business too quickly will erode the relationship. They waste time and socialize excessively. Our electrical rep stops in without an appointment and says, "Hi, Don. It's really good to see you. Last time we talked you were packing your son off to college. How's he doing these days?" . . .

In diagnosing needs they gather a lot of information, but much of it is irrelevant. They are sympathetic listeners, but allow the conversation to wander. "Gosh, I'm sorry to hear that. He just barely missed making the varsity? Tough luck!" . . .

2. Sales presentations

Pleasers' presentations tend to be long and vague. They do not get directly to the point and often omit important, but controversial topics. The salesman's presentation goes something like this: "The company is doing a promotion this month on these new watt-saver fluorescent tubes, and I can get you a special deal. With your kids in college, I'm sure saving money must be important to you." This leaves the prospect spinning, wondering what the relationship is between his college kids and the lamps. Such leaps of logic are typical of the pleaser. They *assume* they know what will please the prospect.

3. Handling objections and closing

Pleasers listen carefully to objections, and their sympathetic concern makes it easy for prospects to share hidden grievances, but their answers go on and on, and they're unable to create the sense of urgency required to overcome stalls.

"Well, we're really happy with the lighting we have right now," says the prospect, "and we won't be ready to re-lamp the showroom for another six months at least."

"That's too bad," says the Pleaser. "I was hoping I could count on you for six cases. You could buy them now and store them until you're ready to re-lamp, and take advantage of this special pricing. I sure hate to see you miss out on this great deal. I'd even be willing to sit on the paperwork for a while to buy you some more time." Great, Mr. Pleaser. You're so anxious to do this prospect a favor that you didn't even *hear* the objection. Obviously the prospect isn't interested in a deal on fluorescent tubes right now.

Getting the order is the Pleaser's greatest weakness. They simply cannot push. *They may not even ask for the order,* and they rarely ask more than once. Asking may turn a pleasant chat into an unpleasant confrontation. "Is there anything else you need today?" they ask.

"No, we're in good shape."

"Okay, I'll check back with you in a few months when you're ready to re-lamp. Sure would like to have your business." The Pleaser salesperson leaves empty-handed.

4. After-sale tracking

Pleasers track better than the other types because they would rather call on existing customers than risk rejection by contacting new ones. They genuinely care about their customers' welfare and may be very good at maintaining a portfolio of regulars, but they have difficulty selling new accounts.

Pleaser salespeople satisfy a very important need: they really care about their prospects' welfare. Although their warmth and need for reciprocal warmth will turn off extremely Ego- and Authority-phase prospects, everyone else appreciates their concern, *even if they don't buy.*

Pleasers are most effective selling commodity products (such as coal, steel, lumber, and automobile parts) on a repeat basis. They lack the forcefulness needed to get quick sales from strangers and do not have enough objectivity to analyze complex problems. But they can build strong relationships with customers who want good after-sales service.

Authority *salespeople*

Not many salespeople are extremely Authority-based. They feel uncomfortable with the emotional aspects of selling, so they treat it as an intellectual exercise, a "numbers game." Their approach is logical, fact-oriented, and no-pressure. Authority salespeople assume that people will logically buy the product that best fits their needs and ignore the irrational factors that influence buying decisions.

1. Recon and initial approach

The Authority recon is usually excellent. They often spend *too much* time doing analyses and planning, since they would rather plan than call on people.

Their approach is professional, businesslike, impersonal, and does not build rapport. Their concentration on facts and data turns off many prospects. This electrical supply rep explains, "Our new watt-saver fluorescent lamp uses 17 percent less energy than ordinary forty-watt tubes with the same lumen output."

Their diagnosis of the prospect's criteria needs is always thorough. They listen carefully, try to get all the facts, and take the time to organize them into a coherent picture, but they don't learn much about priorities and problems. "If you tell me what your average electric consumption has been over the least three months, I can work up a pay-back point."

2. Sales presentations

Their sales talks are factual and logical, but lack emotional appeal. They tend to be drawn out, tedious, and often sound more like a lecture. "This energy differential is made possible by a new phosphor coating, which becomes excited at a lower voltage threshold, so the cathodes don't have to burn as hot." The prospect thinks, "Huh?" Great, Mr. Authority. You've just told your prospect that he's *stupid*.

3. Handling objections and closing

Authority salespeople analyze objections carefully and provide all the information needed to answer the easy ones. However, they can't handle stalls and hidden objections. They do not probe effectively for hidden objections because they don't understand their emotional basis.

"I don't think we want to tear up our showroom just now to re-lamp. It would make a terrible mess," objects the prospect.

"Yes, but the new lamps would pay for themselves in less than eighteen months," says Authority, losing this argument *and* this customer.

Closing is the greatest weakness of the Authority phase. They assume prospects will make logical decisions, so they hesitate to ask, and once they are turned down, they rarely ask again. Stalling is *so* illogical that they just can't understand it. They walk away from procrastinators in disbelief, empty-handed.

"Very well. Thank you for your time. Call us if you change your mind." Exit stage left.

4. After-sale tracking

Authority tracking is systematic and meticulous, but impersonal. Although they see that orders are prepared and delivered properly and that all services are provided as promised, they do not develop an individual relationship with their customers. They pay close attention to the *business* bond, but ignore the more important *human* bond.

"The last time we talked, on June twelfth, around ten o'clock, you suggested you might be interested in converting to our watt-saver fluorescent lamps. Do you still have an interest?" You can guess what the answer to *that* question will be.

Although classic Authority-phase people rarely succeed at sales, most salespeople could use more professional aloofness. It would help them to analyze prospects' problems and their own selling styles more objectively. Indifference becomes more valuable as the analytic elements of the sale increase. Authority people usually fail at selling simple consumer products, but may be quite successful selling capital equipment, industrial real estate, engineering services, and other sophisticated items.

Principle *salespeople: True guerrillas*

1. Recon and initial approach

The salesperson operating in the Principle phase plans carefully, applying guerrilla marketing[2] principles to find the people who are most likely to want or need their products. Guerrillas marshal their efforts in those markets. They are systematic, but not excessive, scheduling their time in loose blocks, allowing themselves to be spontaneous.

Their approach is courteous, direct, and businesslike. They care about their prospect's personal as well as professional life, and demonstrate that they've done their homework. For the guerrilla, determining the Need, Budget, and level of Commitment are the most critical parts of the call.

The electrical rep opens with a businesslike statement of purpose:

[2]We recommend Jay Conrad Levinson's several *Guerrilla Marketing* books to every aspiring guerrilla. Call Guerrilla Marketing International at 1-800-748-6444.

"Hello, Mr. Prospect. Thank you for taking time to meet with me today. I'd like to ask you a few questions."

As Stephen Covey suggests in his book *The Seven Habits of Highly Effective People*[3], they "seek first to understand, then to be understood." The secret is that they ask a lot of questions and really listen to discover the true needs under the superficial ones. Guerrillas seek out the real budget behind the generalized "we can afford anything you can build" type of statement. And guerrillas listen carefully to find out exactly how contracts and purchases are made at each firm.

2. Sales presentations

The Principle presentation is short and direct, relating to the particular personality and unique wants and needs uncovered by the guerrilla. They've learned to ignore everything else. They focus on the solution to the prospect's problem *as the prospect has defined it*. "Okay, as I understand your need, the real problem is getting the right color balance on your plants and flowers; is that what you're concerned about?"

3. Handling objections and closing

Principle salespeople treat objections as legitimate questions, probing for the underlying concern. They assume that prospects are *experts* in their own field, and rely on *their* advice. "I know very little about plants. When you say 'color balance,' what exactly does that mean?" They create an atmosphere of trust and support that makes it easy for prospects to *share* their point of view. A true guerrilla seeks out objections and responds honestly. Chapter 5, "The Needs Stage," gives several examples.

Guerrillas are always closing in. We saw a white convertible BMW heading up to Lake Tahoe one weekend loaded for fun. The license plate told the whole story: CLOZ. Guerrillas close up-front by understanding the needs and the budget of the prospect. When they make their presentation, they align it with something to which the prospect is *already* committed. "I'm beginning to appreciate your concern. These watt-saver lamps actually have a slightly warmer color than the ones you're using, so red roses and pink azaleas will look brighter, and foliage will look healthier to your customers."

[3] Stephen R. Covey, *The Seven Habits of Highly Effective People* (New York: Simon & Schuster, 1989)

4. After-sale tracking

Guerrillas' tracking is meticulous, bordering on fanatical. They reward every customer by doing something extra, something unexpected. "I'd like to leave a set of four of these lamps for you to experiment with. Please let me know how they work in your showroom so I can share your findings with other customers." They take personal responsibility for making sure *everything* is delivered as specified and that it works as expected. They consider this service part of their commitment to the customer relationship.

The guerrilla challenge

Your own cognitive priorities may conflict with your income criteria. Actions that make you comfortable may bother prospects. You must, therefore, understand your own needs and adapt to the needs of each prospect you meet.

Your personality can help you make sales as well. From *Principle*, *Responsible*, and *Universal* phases, all of the resources of the *Ego*, *Pleaser*, and *Authority* are available to you. The *Ego* phase provides that indispensable drive to win, and the tenacity to close again and again. It helps you meet strangers and push for the order. The *Pleaser* phase helps you build relationships and makes your influence and aloofness less irritating. The *Authority* phase helps you analyze prospects' problems and see a clearer picture.

Guerrillas operating out of the *Principle* phase have a compelling charisma. They can shift from *Ego* to *Pleaser* to *Authority* to *Principle* phases as the situation requires. Most people look forward to being with them. They are welcomed into the prospect's territory with open arms. And that makes the job of selling a whole lot easier.

5
The Need Stage

Priorities and criteria

A guerrilla in San Francisco suspected from their first telephone conversation that this Bank of America vice president was a classic *Authority* phase prospect. Her condescending tone and direct manner said *Authority*. Meeting her that morning confirmed it.

In the first few minutes, she openly boasted that she had sent all the competitors running. In her own words, she was "unsalable."

As a guerrilla, he could anticipate her reaction to salespeople as well as her hidden agenda. He also knew what the best approach would be. As a result of his knowing *more* about what she really needed than *she* did, she became one of his best clients.

This chapter explains the *Need Stage*, the first of the six steps of NaB & CaPTuRe, the acronym that guides all guerrillas in the guerrilla sales cycle.

The objective of the *Need Stage* is to verify, up-front, that your product or service matches, or is very close to matching, your prospect's wants or needs. If there isn't a match, the guerrilla asks for referrals and exits, saving everyone's time. A guerrilla closes at the beginning, right up-front, rather than at the end. The key to up-front closing is actively listening. Many salespeople assume they know what prospects need and are impatient to start selling, but they don't listen adequately. While they may present their product in an attractive way, their presentations lack the critical connection between their product and the prospects' wants, needs, and budget.

There are two major purposes for listening: to get information and to make prospects receptive to your ideas. People are hungry for understanding. They think nobody cares. When you listen carefully and show you sincerely want to understand, prospects will relax, talk freely, and welcome your recommendations.

You must learn about your prospects' problems, the resources available to solve them, other solutions being considered, and many other facts in order to plan an effective personalized presentation, answer objections effectively, and write orders. **In addition, you must uncover at least one objection or problem.** This will be used later at the end of the *Transaction Stage*. Finding at least one objection is necessary to complete the six-stage *NaB & CaPTuRe Track*.

The techniques used to acquire this information can either develop or detract from your relationship. Prospects will trust you and look forward to your presentation if they feel you understand and want to help. Unless both objectives are achieved, a sale is unlikely. You cannot make an effective presentation without this information, and you can't create a desire to buy unless prospects trust you and listen receptively.

By completing the Need Stage, the guerrilla avoids one of the most common objections to making a buying decision: "I'm really not sure we could use it. Let me think it over."

Meeting new people

Okay, you've scouted out a prospect and you have an appointment. You walk into your prospect's office, she rises to meet you, and you extend your hand. Now what do you do?

For starters, give yourself space. When you walk into a room, stop momentarily at the doorway and scan the room for a second or two before entering.

The handshake

Now comes the moment of the all-important handshake. The handshake has been used as a greeting for longer than we can remember, and no doubt, it originally meant, "See, I'm unarmed, you can trust me." But it's evolved over thousands of years until today it conveys a number of subtle messages, each communicated by slight differences in touch, pressure, and force.

The most important thing to remember about the handshake is to make sure that you get *hold* of the prospect's hand correctly. Most "dead fish" handshakes happen accidentally, because you're looking the person in the eye, walking, talking, and not paying attention to how you're clasping their outstretched hand. The guerrilla thing to do is to offer the open hand with the palm turned down slightly, and then, at the moment of touch, push away gently against the fleshy part at the base of the thumb until it's made a good contact, "web to web." Then fold your fingers gently around the prospect's hand. This slight delay communicates confidence and avoids the accidental limp-wristed slip-grip.

Ego is communicated by two elements: the degree of *grip* and the *tilt* in the handshake. If you intend to communicate dominance, grip the hand firmly when you shake it, but avoid the bone-crusher. Excessive pressure communicates insecurity. Pressing down gently with the thumb instead will tilt the handshake down slightly on the prospect's side, and slightly up on your side, putting the prospect a tad off-balance and creating a feeling of your being taller.

You can also use *push-pull* to communicate dominance, by pushing your hand away slightly, increasing your personal space. If done carefully, these techniques can telegraph subliminal signals that create an advantage with a potential Ego-phase adversary or neutralize differences in age, status, size, or gender.

You can put your Pleaser-phase prospect at ease by doing the *opposite*. By tilting the handshake *toward* you, you can convey subordination, friendliness, or the relinquishing of control. A simultaneous *ancillary touch* with the left hand denotes familiarity and history, even with strangers, and is very effective when greeting Pleaser-phase prospects. The most common form of ancillary touch is the two-handed handshake, which communicates intimacy, and the farther up their arm you touch, the more familiar the message. The *degree* of intimacy is communicated by moving the touch *farther up the wrist*, and with someone you have known a long time, you would touch higher up on the forearm, at the elbow, or even on the upper arm. If it feels comfortable and you want to make a new acquaintance feel like an old friend, touch them on the elbow with your left hand while shaking hands with your right. This ancillary touch can be helpful when being introduced by a mutual third party to create an atmosphere of intimacy, in effect, bringing the history of *their* relationship into yours.

Posturing

How you stand during your handshake is also significant. Stepping forward with the right foot is the most common form, and communicates *parity*, mirroring the forward motion of the prospect. For a change, try stepping into the handshake with the *left* foot. Practice on a friend and you'll feel the subtle difference it makes. It makes them reach into your personal space with their outstretched hand and communicates a degree of warmth, acceptance, and trust.

Before taking a seat, always adjust the position of the chair slightly, whether it needs it or not. You're, in effect, taking control of that little bit of real estate. If possible, turn your chair so you can directly face your prospect. Rather than flopping down in the seat, lower yourself vertically onto the edge, then sit back, maintaining your balance.

Guerrillas are also known for their relaxed good humor, so they **never** complain about the weather, the traffic, or the rough day they're having. They have something upbeat to say about the surroundings, the office building, or the receptionist who greeted them.

The important thing to remember is that *everything* you do communicates a message. By being aware of the messages you're telegraphing with your handshake and body posture, you can create the emotional climate you want, rather than leave it to chance.

The opening: Be prepared to be unprepared

The first thing you want to find out is what the prospect had in mind when she agreed to this appointment. You want your prospect to set the agenda for this meeting. Guerrillas resist the temptation to start telling about themselves or their product. This is where you set the stage and establish yourself as a real person, not an overpolished professional.

The guerrilla wants to find out what the client heard on the phone, not what the guerrilla *thinks* was said or understood. An opening used by a guerrilla in Chicago accomplishes this beautifully.

He sat down and began, "I didn't get a chance to go by the office this morning to pick up your file. What was it, specifically, that we were going to discuss today?" The prospect replied with, "Well, you said that your firm sold insulation, and our heating bills are going sky high." This guerrilla interrupts with "That sounds important. Do you mind if I take a few notes?" and begins listening actively as his prospect outlines the meeting.

For the guerrilla, the big questions are: what does this prospect really *want*, and what does she *think* she *needs?* These questions are important because people buy what they *want*, not *necessarily* what they need. This basic truth of human nature is often overlooked. Please don't misunderstand. You have a professional obligation to solve their problem, that is, to satisfy their *physical criteria*. But people are motivated by wants, and there may be little connection between the want and the need.

Order takers operating in the Pleaser phase sell only to needs, while high-pressure Egos sell only to wants. The guerrilla creates a major strategic advantage by selling to *both*.

Building credibility

Guerrillas know that, *ultimately, buying is an act of faith* for the prospect. The decision depends on whether they believe in the product *and* the salesperson. Even though the process occurs unconsciously, there are four "C" factors that affect credibility.

1. Consistency

The first factor people weigh is prior experience. Have you been *consistent* with them in the past, and how so? If you tell someone that you're putting the information in the mail today, then it's important that you do just that. If you've been nasty to a coworker and decide to butter them up a bit because you need a favor, they'll be suspicious from the first kind word you utter. Guerrillas are consistent.

2. Credibility

The second trust factor for a guerrilla is credibility. What *story* are you telling your audience? Think about the way you'll be introduced and the story you'll tell about yourself. Guerrillas never exaggerate.

3. Congruency

The third trust factor is congruency. Do all the pieces of your story and image fit together with your *identity*? You'd be suspicious of someone driving an expensive sports car and wearing rags. Given an incongruent message, people are far more likely to believe the nonverbal components of the message: your posture, voice tone, inflection, and so on.

4. Common ground

You can also build trust by establishing a common ground. This is a very powerful rapport builder. When you're away from home, have you ever noticed how you feel when you see a license plate from your home state? You spontaneously feel something in common with these people.

Try to discover some small thing you share in common with every prospect. Even something trivial will do, but it's especially effective if you share a common interest. Ask where they're from, or where they went to school. Are they sports fans? Do they have a special skill or hobby, or a favorite charity? To arouse prospects' interest, guerrillas talk about what prospects are *most* interested in — themselves.

Criteria and priorities

Guerrillas know that people do not buy features and benefits. They buy solutions to problems. The world's best product or service is worthless if it doesn't satisfy a need. As a guerrilla, your task is to discover your prospects' physical criteria and demonstrate how your product or service satisfies them. You'll earn their confidence when you show that you are meeting both their physical *and* emotional needs and that you can relate to them on their terms.

You must create a positive relationship before your prospects will answer questions or even listen to your presentation. You won't be able to identify your prospects' criteria and they will not be receptive to your solution unless you satisfy their priorities as well.

Satisfying your prospects' physical criteria is far more important than satisfying their cognitive priorities. In fact, satisfying their priorities is only a means to this end. Concentrating on your prospects' cognitive priorities while ignoring their physical criteria may increase your popularity, but it will not lead to increased business. People buy solutions. They do not buy because you are smart or nice or clever.

Almost all salespeople repeatedly violate this principle. They either concentrate on being a great person or focus on the product's specifications. They talk about what their product is, how it works, and how it compares with the competition, but not what it will do for their prospects.

Even experienced salespeople who take the problem-solving approach tend to deal with criteria in a superficial way. They often address only specifications that are directly related to their product, and ignore subtler, more important priorities.

For example, a computer salesperson might tell a prospect that he needs a faster, '486-based machine with a 100-megabyte hard disk to process a rapidly growing database. This may be true, but it doesn't go far enough. A computer is just a tool, and data are analyzed for a purpose. Sensitive guerrillas get *beyond* the prospect's data processing requirements to learn *why* the database is growing so rapidly and why this prospect feels it's a priority. They strive to discover what the prospect wants the business to become, and how the computer can help it grow. The actual physical specifications of the new system, the *criteria*, will be determined later.

You can do exactly the same. Find out where your prospects want to go and what obstacles are preventing them from getting there. Then show how your product or service can help them reach their goals.

Prospects face myriad challenges every day. They're called upon to solve problems with money and machinery, with engineering and electronics, with communications and commitments, with designs and decisions, with people and personalities. Whether they acknowledge it or not, they are probably overworked, overstressed, and overwhelmed. Demonstrate a sensitivity to their situation. First, show that you'll be *fair* with them, that you really *care*, and that your job is to *share* in solving these difficulties. They will be much more receptive to your proposal.

Things to look for

Many salespeople ask questions only about direct opportunities to sell their products; they focus entirely on prospects' direct needs and ability to pay. This narrow focus reduces prospects' receptivity and prevents you from learning what they really want. Prospects will feel you're not interested in their welfare. They'll view you as another hustler, hungry for a quick commission. You may be so intent on discovering a need for one product that you overlook a much larger sale. The more you know about your prospects, the better your chances. Guerrillas relate to prospects as people, not just as potential buyers.

Evaluation of proposals

Your prospect may have explicit written criteria for evaluating proposals and for making buying commitments. Probe for these criteria.

Find out how proposals will be evaluated. If there is a formal request for proposal, study it carefully before the call, make margin notes, and ask some searching questions. Learn exactly what prospects want and how they intend to evaluate these proposals. Your presentation must then explicitly compare your product to their specified criteria.

You may learn that their evaluation process favors your competition. For example, they may not care about some of your product's features, but be very price conscious. If your competition offers a cheaper but less desirable product, then you're at a severe disadvantage. Ask about the *rationale* behind the standards. Ask how and why these criteria were established, and try to add value to the proposal to make it more competitive. If you can't change the criteria, your competitor will probably get the business.

Alternate solutions

What other solutions are they considering? Doing nothing is frequently an option; are they considering doing nothing? Are they thinking of buying a totally different kind of product or a similar product from one of your competitors? Learn as much as you can about their options. Then convince them that your solution is better.

Fear of buying

Prospects can be afraid of many things, such as buying something they don't need, being ignored after the sale, or offending their bosses. They may be so intimidated by their problems that they can't discuss them openly.

As long as these fears remain hidden, you are helpless to reduce their impact. Help prospects discuss them openly. The techniques presented in the next section will relax most prospects and help them discuss their fears.

Listen actively and visibly

If prospects feel you are really listening, they will do their best to help you understand. They will open up, talk frankly, and even forgive and correct your misunderstandings.

Listening is an active and visible process. You should let prospects know how hard you are working to understand them. A few simple techniques will increase the flow of information from prospects and your understanding of that information.

Concentrate like crazy

Put everything else out of your mind. Forget your domestic problems, your next appointment, expense reports, and hunger pains. Concentrate on this prospect. Concentrate intensely. You will learn more, and prospects will recognize and appreciate your concern.

Pause along the way

Silence may make you uncomfortable, but it's part of the required discipline of the guerrilla. If you are talking, the prospect can't talk. So pause frequently to encourage prospects to comment, and make those pauses long enough. Many prospects are slow responders. A long pause gives them a chance to organize their thoughts and then clearly state what's on their minds.

Let the prospect see you take notes

Note-taking demonstrates that you're listening carefully. It also helps you to see patterns. Facts may seem isolated when you hear them, but a review of your notes can reveal unsuspected patterns. Record only the important points. Do not become so intent on recording details that prospects feel you are not relating personally.

Ask permission before starting to take notes. A few prospects feel uncomfortable about note-taking, and they will appreciate your courtesy.

Maintain eye contact

Look at your prospects in a warm, nonchallenging way. Let your eyes show you genuinely understand.

The About-Face

One of the reasons for the public's negative view of salespeople is that they tend to do all the talking. You can't miss the "Tell ya what I'm gonna do!" stereotype. This all too typical loudmouth is a blight on the profession. The guerrilla lets prospects do most of the talking and uses the About-Face to keep the sales interview moving toward the order.

This purely guerrilla strategy involves asking questions in response to a prospect's questions and concerns. We call this strategy the About-Face because it's 180 degrees from the typical sales response. What does an About-Face do for modern guerrillas?

While you are asking the questions, your prospect is doing most of the talking. Your questions shift the focus away from you and flatter your prospect. Your About-Face questions help your prospect to clearly define and, perhaps, answer their own objections. Your questions help you gather additional information to support your presentation, and they help you to probe for your prospect's cognitive needs and priorities.

Ask three times

Prospects rarely give a straight answer up-front. Guerrillas know the counseling principle of three; that is, it will probably take three questions along the same line to get to the prospect's real intent. Their first two answers generally arise out of the Authority phase, and are intellectual, factual, and logical. The third answer is usually an emotional response that reflects the prospect's true intent. The prospect reasons that since you took the time, had the patience, and showed enough interest to ask three times, you must sincerely want to know. Perhaps the prospect can trust the honesty of your questioning.

Here's an example of an About-Face: The prospect says, "I need top quality. Can you give me a high-quality product?"

The guerrilla response is "When you say 'high quality,' exactly what specifications do you require?"

By asking this kind of question, you'll find out a lot more than if you launch into an explanation about your quality control. When you *think* you know what your prospect needs, watch out.

"The price is too high"

Notice that this common objection is a *statement*, not a question. This is true with most objections. The prospect is trying to *tell* you something rather than ask you something. That's why guerrillas never *answer* objections. They don't require answers. However, the prospect *is* looking for a response.

The guerrilla replies by asking, *"When you say 'too high,' what do you propose?"* or, *"When you say 'too high,' relative to what?"*

There is no way for you to know what the prospect *means* by saying, "The price is too high." There's a big difference between a statement and an objection. The statement "the price is too high" may be the prospect's way of dealing with an issue totally unrelated to you or your product. This is not necessarily an invitation to compromise. Using an About-Face gives validity to the prospect's statement and lets you hear what was meant. Take the key words, the subject nouns or verb, and reflect them back in a question.

"Your price is too high."

"*Too high . . .?*" (pause, expectant look)

"We're going to have to talk about lowering your prices if you want my business."

"Okay, and when you say '*your business*,' what exactly do you have in mind?"

"I want to throw all of our catalog business to you."

"By '*catalog business*,' how much are we talking about?"

"About ten thousand dollars a month."

"'*Ten thousand a month?*' So, we are talking about a whole different price list, then?"

"Yes, and another thing . . ."

Now the guerrilla has gotten to the *real* issue, *volume pricing*. A less courageous salesperson would have tried to answer the objection by pitching quality or service or competitiveness. It requires boldness to ricochet the objection back to the prospect for clarification.

Here are some more examples of About-Faces with prospects:

"Your deliveries are too slow."

"What does '*too slow*' mean for your firm's needs?"

"I'm really unhappy about this situation."

"When you say '*unhappy*,' what does that imply?"

"Does this come in blue?"

"Why is *blue* of interest to you?"

"How wide is it?"

"Why do you ask about the *width?*"

"I'm concerned about it fitting in our storage area."

"Great! Let's measure the space very carefully."

"We really like your firm, and we are giving you top consideration for this new contract. When can we see your proposal?"

What is this prospect trying to say by "top consideration"? Who knows? The guerrilla does an About-Face:

"First of all, thank you. Let me ask a question. When you say '*top consideration*,' what do you intend?"

The exception to the About-Face

If a prospect asks the *identical* question twice, answer it quickly with facts, figures, and logic! You're dealing with a pure Authority-phase prospect.

Universal criteria

There are a few things that *everyone* is interested in. Virtually everyone is interested in *saving time, saving money,* and *reducing headaches.* Because these criteria are universal, the guerrilla strives constantly to satisfy them as a matter of course, whether the prospect has indicated they are important or not.

Time

Consultants preach the gospel of competing in time. We have instant coffee, instant oatmeal, instant *everything.* Prospects have been conditioned by technology to expect instant results. They don't want to wait on hold. They don't want to wait until "sometime this afternoon" for someone to return their call. They don't want to wait until next week to get a delivery. They don't want to stand in line. No matter what it is, they want it NOW.

So the guerrilla is constantly looking for ways to *shorten cycle times,* to respond to the customer more quickly, to satisfy this need by cutting a day here, an hour there. Guerrillas always respect the prospects' time and never waste it. Guerrillas never keep people waiting if it can be helped, and when it can't be helped, they keep the delay under twenty minutes or renegotiate the appointment. People will wait about twenty minutes before they reach the threshold of impatience.

Guerrillas are quick and decisive. Guerrillas call instead of writing, use fax instead of mail. If you say you will call at ten, wait until the *stroke* of ten o'clock, creating the impression that you conduct *all* of your business with the same split-second precision. Prospects will be more likely to keep appointments and commitments with you in the future.

Make a point to be exactly on time for the first meeting or interview. *Establish the time frame* when you set the appointment, letting the prospect know about how long the meeting will take, verify it very early in your conversation, and stick to it. If you can get your message across in *three* minutes instead of the thirty you've scheduled, prospects will appreciate your efforts, and tend to move things along more quickly in their dealings with you in the future.

Money

Prospects want to *save money*. It's the name of the game in business. Anything they can do to cut costs makes their business more profitable. The guerrilla keeps this in mind, knowing that most of his competitors sell on the basis of price. But there are many other ways a product or service can influence the customer's bottom line: cost of handling, storage, inventory, financing, or the impact it has on other areas of operation, like extended terms that free up cash. Any of these can cost-justify a higher price. The following chapter, "The Budget Stage," expands these ideas in detail.

Headaches

Prospects also want to make their lives less complicated. They want to *reduce headaches*. Countless firms pay a premium price for their office supplies because they can get everything from one vendor who delivers and bills them monthly. Some firms have sued to cancel multimillion dollar contracts because a supplier was one day late with a critical part, forcing them to close down their line. Prospects dislike detail, paperwork, and complications. They want it to be simple and easy. The guerrilla constantly tries to make it no hassle, no paperwork, no problem.

Frito-Lay has cornered the mom-and-pop-store market for snack foods by having its salespeople take care of product inventory, stocking, and rotation.

A dry cleaner in Wichita put in a drive-thru window, gave its regular customers numbered laundry bags, and directly bills their credit cards. No worries. From pizza to pencils to plastics, "We deliver" has become the battle cry of guerrilla operators.

Priority words

The keys to the prospects' emotional needs are found in their *priority words*. These words can show you how this individual is going to make the decision. Priority words are also the ammunition guerrillas use to defend their proposals against the competition, and the prospect will provide a clip-full if you really listen.

If you really listen, people will tell you *exactly* what they *need* and exactly what they *want* from you. You might have a hundred good reasons why they should do what you're suggesting, but their decision will ultimately hinge on three of four factors that *they* feel are compelling. Guerrillas always sell to these priorities. The priority words will tell you what those factors will be.

What do you want?

Priority words are found in the prospects' answers to questions like "What do you want in a _____?" (car, house, computer) or "What are you looking for from your _____?" (insurance company, real estate agent, stockbroker). Listen closely to the answers and jot down the key words, the *adjectives* and *adverbs* that describe the prospect's priorities. Then *probe* those issues, using the *same words* to frame your question.

For example, consider a familiar situation like buying a car. The priority question here is: "What do you look for in a car?" Your answer will contain your priority words. Your priorities for buying a car might include "style, comfort, and good gas mileage." Let's look at the last one. What do people mean when they say "good gas mileage"? Twenty, thirty-five, fifty miles per gallon? It depends! And the guerrilla has no way of knowing whether twenty-eight miles per gallon on the highway will cause the prospect to view the car for sale as an economy model or a gas hog. But if the guerrilla describes the car as "having good gas mileage for such a comfortable car," matching the *criteria words* offered by the prospect, the car is much more likely to be perceived in a favorable light.

Take another example. A guerrilla selling a printing service might ask, "What do you look for in selecting a printer?" The prospect's response will reflect the priorities the prospect uses to make that choice. The factors the prospect mentions will be significant to the decision, and the guerrilla can safely ignore everything else. The prospect might say, "I look for good service and timeliness. I also carefully check the quality, and of course, price is always a factor."

These words, "*service, timeliness, quality,* and *price,*" are this prospect's priority words, and we will note them carefully.

An important thing to keep in mind about priority words is that *you don't know what they mean.* The guerrilla has no idea exactly what this prospect means when he says "service." What's "service"? For you, it might mean you'd rather stand in line than be waited on by someone who's rushed and surly. The prospect's standards and expectations might be very different from your own. But the guerrilla really doesn't have to know the prospect's expectations, because the prospect *does*. He knows what "service" means to him, and the guerrilla knows it's *meaningful*, so if you use it in your presentation, he'll translate it for you and attach the appropriate value.

If the guerrilla promises quick turnaround, that may have meaning for the prospect, and it may not. But if the guerrilla says, "We pride ourselves on providing really first-rate *service*; you can count on us to *service* your account," that's going to communicate, because that's a priority word. The prospect knows what it means, and the guerrilla knows it's important to him.

The same thing is true of the priority for timeliness. What does timeliness mean? At this point, it really doesn't matter, because the prospect knows what it means for him. And because he offered it as a priority word, it's likely to trigger a positive feeling that will play a role in his decision. Even if you don't really know what meaning a prospect's priority words have for him, you can use them to get his attention and evoke a positive, receptive attitude.

The guerrilla might say, "I represent a printer whose *service* is impeccable, and the *quality* is the highest I have seen. Their *price* isn't cheap, but if I understand you correctly, you wouldn't want a cheap printer. The turnaround on the job is always *timely*. Would you be interested in doing business with a firm like that?" How can he say no?

Notice the use of the words "service," "quality," and "price." When you echo your prospects' priority words you will see their attention focus. They may nod their head up and down, or their faces may flush a bit as they relax and become receptive. Priority words are powerful rapport builders.

No mind reading, please

Two points. First, don't try to second-guess what prospects mean by their priority words, and second, don't try to substitute your own vocabulary for theirs. You run the risk that your choice of words won't have the same meaning for them as they do for you.

Ultimately, the guerrilla is going to have to deliver on what those words mean, but you are not quite ready to do that yet. In order to sell printing to this individual, you're going to have to prove that your service is as good as his standards. You'll have to prove that you can deliver on a timely basis, which means you eventually have to find out what his deadline is. You'll have to demonstrate that your quality is going to meet his expectations, and you may have to ask him for samples of other work he has had done so that you can establish what that standard is. Certainly, you are going to have to come to some agreement on the price.

What priority words do is give the guerrilla the keys to unlock the prospect's decision-making strategy. Now we know exactly where to probe and expand. But at this point, you can engage the prospect's interest simply by asking the question "What do you want in a _____?" listening for the nouns, the priority words, and then systematically *assuring the prospect in advance* that you can deliver those things.

Forget it

Guerrillas also know that *they can safely ignore everything other than the prospect's priorities.* If you can address the priorities based on what the prospect has told you, and *confine yourself to those issues*, then you've simplified the task for both of you.

A real estate guerrilla might ask, "What do you want in a new home?"

The prospect responds with "We'd like someplace warm and cozy that will give us some privacy."

"What is it about being *cozy* that's important to you?"

"This city is just so cold and impersonal, we don't have any room to entertain, and there are times when we just want to be totally alone together."

Now it's time to verify our understanding of their priorities. "So what you're telling me is that you want something *private*, away from the city, perhaps out in the woods or in the country. You want a place that *feels small and cozy*, but with some room to entertain friends. Is that right?" Always finish with a question.

"Yes, but not too far from the city. We still have to commute."

The magic selling questions

Some helpful questions for isolating priority words include:

"What is the biggest discomfort you currently face?"

"What role do others play in creating this problem?"

"What other problems do you have with that?"

"What other ideas do you have?"

"If you could have things any way you wished, what would you change?"

"How would this affect the current situation?"

"Why would you want to change?"

"Do you have a preference?"

"Is there anything else you can tell me?"

The answers to these and similar questions will provide the keys to your prospect's motivation.

How does that look?

"How does *cozy* look to you?" Now the guerrilla makes the transition from subjective or emotional *priorities* to *physical criteria*, asking the prospects to define their feelings as physical specifications.

"We'd like to have a fireplace in the living room, and picture windows that open onto a great view."

"And a deck, with a spa, where we could barbecue or just relax alone."

"Okay, I'm beginning to get the picture. Maybe two bedrooms, two baths. Well insulated. Maybe a fireplace in the master bedroom as well?"

Criteria words

The prospect will also have a set of physical specifications that the product or service must meet, as in "it absolutely, positively has to be there overnight," or "I'm looking for a dress in a size seven." These criteria must ultimately be met in order for the prospect to be satisfied. The guerrilla listens for these *criteria words* as well, and notes them throughout the interview. Three very powerful magic questions for isolating criteria words are:

"What are you using now?"

"What do you like *most* about it?"

"What do you like *least* about it?"

These answers tell the guerrilla what they *have*, what they want to *keep*, and what they want to *change*, while avoiding a direct query into their problem.

Once guerrillas have isolated the prospect's key priorities and criteria, they concentrate on those issues and ignore everything else. Other criteria may be introduced as the conversation continues, but the guerrilla concentrates only on the priority and criteria words isolated by the prospect.

The guerrilla understands that *people do things for their reasons, not yours.* You may have a hundred good reasons why they should buy this particular mountain home: price, location, good roads, rapid appreciation, close to schools, shops, recreation. And you know what? They couldn't care less. No matter how good your reasons may be, ultimately, the prospect's reasons will prevail. The guerrilla saves ammunition by aiming at the priorities and criteria defined by the prospect's answers.

Progression

It's also useful to isolate the *steps* the prospect follows when making a decision. People have a methodology they follow when making decisions, and this strategy, or *progression*, is unique for each prospect, but they tend to use the *same* progression *whenever* they make a decision. The question that you can use to elicit *progression* is to ask, "How did you decide . . . ?" For example, a real estate agent might ask a couple, "How did you decide to move into the house where you live now?" then listen to the *sequence* of steps.

"Well, *first* we narrowed the search down to a particular neighborhood where we wanted to live, *then* we checked all the listings, marking each address on a map. *Then* we looked at each one until we found the one that felt right."

This answer reveals not only the criteria, but the progression of the couple's house-buying strategy. If you *lead* them through the *same* progression, it makes it easy for them to buy from you. Start by "narrowing down" to the particular neighborhoods they like best, then pull out a map and start "marking." Like a familiar chair, following their progression puts you in the selling "groove." It fits their nature and their temperament. Besides, they're going to buy the house *their way* anyway. If not from you, then from someone who makes them feel comfortable. So you might as well match their strategy. Listen for the structure of the process they follow when making a similar decision, then systematically structure your case using the same progression.

Does that compute?

Sometimes customers don't really *know* what they want. Let's say you're a computer salesperson who asks a prospect, "What do you want in a computer?" The response is something like "I don't know" or "I'm not sure." To get the prospect's criteria, you can ask, "What are you using now? What do you like most about that?" or "What's the exact problem you're trying to solve?"

"What are you doing now?" you say.

"We're doing everything manually."

"What do you like most about doing that manually?" you ask, repeating the prospect's words in an About-Face.

"I like the idea that we have in-house control. I like the idea that I can get the reports quickly."

Now we're getting criteria language: *control, in-house, quickly.* If you can show her that your computer will do it more quickly, give her better *control*, and still keep it *in-house*, she's going to buy the computer. And she really doesn't care how many k's of RAM it has, or how many megabytes the disk drives will store, or what its CPU clock speed is, so long as she is in "control." You can ignore the rest, because when you elicit the prospect's criteria, you're asking for a value judgment, and the progression will reveal the *way* they make judgments in that particular context.

You also have to keep in mind that priorities, criteria, and progression are sensitive to the *context* in which they're used. They are non-transferrable. You don't go about buying office supplies in the same way you shop for real estate.

Here are some additional questions for isolating criteria:

"What is your main objective?"

"What are you doing to deal with that situation?"

"What are your plans for the future?"

"How do you plan to get it done?"

"Can you tell me more about that?"

"Is there a deadline?"

The answers to these questions will provide the performance specifications for your proposal. Whatever else this new home may have going for it, it must satisfy these physical criteria.

General and specific priorities

You'll notice that the guerrilla, in addition to satisfying physical criteria, is satisfying emotional priorities as well. There are two major categories of emotional priorities. General priorities common to nearly all prospects, and specific priorities, unique to each type of prospect.

Surveys consistently show that customers want salespeople to relate to them in a certain way, which can best be described as being fair, caring, and willing to share. Guerrillas are familiar with these principles, since they form the bases of being at the *Principle* phase. This becomes a three-way test: "Am I really being fair? Am I showing that I care? Am I willing to do my share, and maybe more?"

Five questions for every guerrilla

The following five questions will help you evaluate how well you are relating to the prospect's general priorities.

1. Do I ask questions that show I really care?

Prospects want this most of all. They want to do business with people who respect them and genuinely care about their welfare. The most important message you can communicate is "I care!"

Consider the way people choose a doctor. Most of us have no way of knowing how competent a particular physician may be. Instead, we choose one who takes a sincere interest, who asks lots of questions, who is careful and complete in his or her diagnosis, and who shows empathy for our discomfort and pain.

When you communicate a sincere concern, prospects will forgive many errors. If they get the impression that you're only interested in the commission, it doesn't make much difference if you do everything else right. They will not trust you and they will not buy.

2. Do I really listen to the answers?

Prospects want to be understood. People are hungry for understanding; they need a sympathetic listener. Many lawyers and accountants spend more time listening and advising people on personal problems than they do working on purely legal or accounting matters.

In order to demonstrate that you've really heard your prospect, summarize their answers by restating. Be explicit and complete. Consult your notes.

"What I heard you saying is . . ."

"If I understand you correctly . . ."

"So, in other words you need . . . and you need it by October second."

Take time to hear them out, even if the conversation seems irrelevant to your business. Prospects will look forward to your next call and will do everything possible to keep you coming back. They will provide the information you need, and they may even buy your products when a competitor's are superior.

3. Do I give my prospect control over the sales meeting?

Prospects fear being out of control, not being in charge of their own lives. We clam up when we suspect we're being manipulated or forced, and in a sales meeting we're particularly on guard. A guerrilla way to sidestep this feeling is to find at least one objection in the Need Stage and invite the prospect to end the meeting right there.

"Uh-oh, we've got a problem, it doesn't come in green. (pause) Am I finished here?" or "Should I leave now?"

It doesn't matter much which phrase you use, as long as the prospect gets the message that you're willing to have the meeting end if the question you've raised is crucial. We've never seen anyone end the meeting at this juncture. Here's why.

You've been actively listening to your prospect for some time now. You may be the only one who has ever listened this way. By now, the prospect understands that you do care, their needs are more important than yours, and now you're showing that you're fair. Maybe green wasn't so important after all!

4. Do I act professionally?

You are not an order taker. Concentrate on the prospect's priorities, communicate sensitivity and concern, but also command respect for yourself as a professional. Remember being professional does not mean having all the answers. It means having a lot of questions and actively listening.

Honesty and directness are important parts of this professional image. Do not be defensive about being a salesperson or pretend you are making a social call. Prospects feel more comfortable if you clearly communicate that you have called to do business. If you appear comfortable in your role, prospects will usually feel comfortable with you.

5. Do I relate to prospects on their own terms?

Prospects and customers really do believe that they are always right, and even when they're wrong, they're still the customer. They believe you're obligated to sell on their terms, and they resent salespeople who don't. Essentially, all prospects want you to communicate: "You're the boss and I'll do whatever I can to make you comfortable."

Prospects particularly resent someone like you trying to satisfy your needs at their expense. It doesn't matter whether your needs are to be the star, to get a warm reaction, or to avoid emotions. Prospects are just not interested in your attempts to make yourself comfortable. They expect you to cater to their comfort.

Since all types of prospects want you to adjust, you must understand the specific needs of different types of prospects as well.

Priorities and the Mind Map

People with well-balanced, mature personalities relate to others naturally. Regardless of the circumstances, they behave in ways that make others more comfortable. They exhibit flexibility. Because they are comfortable with themselves and their role, it is easy for them to adjust to the needs of others and to adapt to a variety of situations. However, psychologists and sociologists tell us that fewer than 15 percent of the adult population are consistently operating from the *Principle* phase or higher.

To help you identify the specific priorities of the prospects you are most likely to encounter, we will look at Phases Two, Three, and Four, the classic *Ego, Pleaser,* and *Authority* personalities, in depth and consider how they respond at the Need Stage.

These profiles will help you understand how you should adapt to each type. Most prospects will have more balanced personalities, and you will need to modify your approach accordingly. For an overview of all seven personality phases, refer to chapter 2, "The Mind Map."

Ego prospects

The characteristic cognitive priority of the *Ego* phase prospect is *status*. For them, everything must be the *best!* They are fiercely competitive, and must win at everything; business, golf, even cocktail parties are life-and-death contests. They are compelled to make more money, lower their handicap, and score more points at parties than anyone else.

When they meet a stranger, they want to know: "Am I *better* than this person? Do I make more money, own a larger house, play better golf?"

Classic Ego people are ambitious, tough, aggressive, overbearing, close-minded, antiintellectual, and insensitive. Since everything is a contest, they can't afford to think about other people's feelings. It would distract their attention from the only goal that really matters: winning.

Since winning is so important, Ego people may cut corners. They would rather not lie or cheat because it taints their victory, but a tainted victory is infinitely better than losing. Because they will do anything to win, they assume others do the same. As a result, they often distrust others.

The positive side of Ego is self-esteem. This is the phase that drives us to learn, to grow, and to overcome negative habits. The Ego is what motivates us to stop smoking, improve our diet, or join a health club. You couldn't negotiate a modern freeway without the Ego-phase aspects of personality.

Ego people are impulsive and individualistic. Taking orders, accepting advice, and following instructions compromise their need for control and are, therefore, a kind of defeat. They insist on doing things their way and may break the rules to do so.

They are afraid of sacrifice, afraid of weakness in themselves, and of being a Pleaser to other people. When two Egos meet, it's war. Both feel, internally, "It's either him or me."

They dominate *Pleaser* phase people. Pleasers naturally accept a submissive role, and Ego people dominate and bully them. Some Ego people deliberately surround themselves with people they can easily push around.

Authority people frustrate them. They cannot stand being ignored, and Authority people ignore almost everybody. The Ego people then become more aggressive, causing the others to withdraw further.

Ego reaction to salespeople

Ego prospects distrust salespeople and are afraid of being exploited or defeated. However, many Ego prospects like having salespeople call. They're stimulated by the battle of wits with other Egos and enjoy bullying the Pleasers.

Their unspoken questions about you include: "Are you good enough to get my business? Are you a top producer? Do you earn as much as I do? Are you tough enough to slug it out with me?" Their status-consciousness makes them insist on dealing only with top people. They want the manager, the vice president, or even the president to handle their account.

Ego prospects generally buy from Ego salespeople. They despise and abuse Pleaser salespeople, but occasionally will "throw them a bone" to build up their own esteem and to keep them coming around. They are intimidated by Authority salespeople, so they dislike and avoid them.

Most effective approach for Egos

The guerrilla approach for the *Ego* phase prospect is to show them how your product will give them the competitive edge. This is their number-one priority. Satisfy their criteria by showing them that your product is the newest, most advanced state-of-the-art, top-of-the-line whatever available on the planet today. Price is usually no object. They want the best.

Ego prospects respond to smooth leadership. Wear your best suit. Have your meeting in the lobby of a posh hotel or the best restaurant in town. Let the glitz show.

One guerrilla offered to meet his Ego prospect at the airport, then hired a limo and driver to drive them both to the prospect's office. A guerrilla real estate agent showed his out-of-town prospect an apartment complex by flying over it in a Learjet.

You must prove that you are tough and competent without being challenging. You can play to their need for status and attention by using the formal form of their name, using their titles, and complimenting them at every opportunity. Be careful. Don't get caught being naive about criteria. Instead of "Gee, that's a nice boat," always *qualify* your accolades. "Those Cal 29s are really comfortable, but, without a spinnaker, they're a bit sluggish in light air." Or give only a partial compliment: "That's a great ad, good use of contrasting color." These half-compliments imply a greater depth of knowledge than you may actually have, though hopefully you have a lot.

Pleaser prospects

The characteristic priority of the *Pleaser* phase is approval. They desperately want love, acceptance, and understanding. They're warm, friendly, and sincerely interested in people, happy to be part of a group, and enjoy all forms of socializing. They are good listeners and are sensitive to the needs of others. However, since approval is so critical, these prospects rarely make buying decisions for fear of being criticized.

Pleasers are cooperative and compliant. They go along with others' ideas because they want to be liked. They are givers. They want to help people, especially those who reward them with gratitude and affection.

All these traits make the Pleaser popular. However, classic Pleaser prospects are so insecure that they constantly seek reassurance. Their demands can become so emotionally exhausting that people withdraw. This increases their insecurity and requests for reassurance, causing further withdrawal. This cycle may continue until relationships break down.

Insecurity makes the Pleaser an easy target to exploit. They may go along, even when they suspect they are being taken for a ride. Pleaser people are afraid of being alone, of rejection, and of all forms of conflict or competition. They are also frightened by hostility, especially their own. They want to believe they feel warm toward everyone.

Jealousy is also a serious problem. They're hostile toward anyone who may come between them and the people they like, but they feel guilty about these feelings.

They usually relate well to other Pleaser people. Each satisfies the other's needs, but both may suspect they are giving more than the other, and ask for more than the other can give.

They will allow Ego people to bully and exploit them. The resentment builds until they can no longer suppress it. Then they lash out in very destructive ways like the meek wife who, after years of abuse, murders her tyrannical husband.

Authority phase people really frustrate them. Pleasers want to get close, but the Authority people remain aloof. Pleasers chase them for a while, then give up and look for someone friendlier.

Pleaser reaction to salespeople

Pleasers are the easiest to call on. They will not reject you openly, and many Pleasers enjoy meeting new people. They're chatty and pleasant, but they can also be covert. They're hesitant to openly discuss any issues involving conflict or problems with other people. They may create the impression that they have the authority to act when they do not. They make promises and stall, rather than risk disappointing you by saying no.

Their unspoken feelings about you are: "Do you sincerely care about me? Do you really like me, or are you just being nice to get my business?"

Most effective approach for Pleasers

The guerrilla approach with the Pleaser is to be patient, take time to establish a relationship, and let them know you like them.

Satisfy their need for approval by asking about their family, their vacation, or their new potted plant. They may be so preoccupied by their socializing that they forget about business, so gently turn the discussions to the business at hand.

Pleaser prospects generally buy from people they like, and are fiercely loyal to their friends, actually buying inferior products or paying higher prices to give business to particular people.

Take the buyer in a department store in Hawaii who kept a hot pot of kona coffee brewing for her visitors, for instance. Even if you're not a coffee drinker, you'd better sip a bit and comment on its rich flavor.

Pleasers need to be encouraged and motivated, and appreciate your efforts, provided they believe you are pushing them for their own good. Make specific suggestions and recommendations.

Authority prospects

The classic Authority prospect is afraid of intimacy, dependence, and unpredictability. Their characteristic cognitive need is control. They are more comfortable with things, ideas, or numbers than they are with people. In fact, one of their major reasons for avoiding people is that they are not as predictable as statistics or machines.

They do not understand emotions and try to avoid them. They suppress their own feelings and ignore other people's. They are shy, aloof, impersonal, and uncommunicative.

Authority people like order and predictability. Their desks, homes, and checkbooks are arranged perfectly, and they can be severely upset by minor deviations from their customary routines.

They are independent, but in a different manner than Ego people. They have even less need for company, but do not want to flaunt their power. They readily accept the impersonal jurisdiction of rules and procedures, but avoid people who attempt to control them directly.

Authority people are open-minded about impersonal issues. They like facts and logic and pride themselves on their objectivity. If someone challenges their position, they do not respond angrily. They try to look at the facts objectively and will change their position if the data require. They will argue for the fun of it.

They generally work in fields requiring objective, impersonal analysis, such as chemistry, physics, engineering, accounting, and management sciences. They enjoy this type of work and are most comfortable with the people who enter these fields. Their relationships with other Authority people are comfortable, but distant. They enjoy each other's minds, and neither makes demands upon the other.

They generally buy from Authority salespeople. They dislike the other types, particularly the Ego people. They hate to be pushed and pressured. They regard Egos as poorly informed, emotional bullies and try to avoid them completely.

Authority people feel contempt and hostility toward Pleaser people. They regard Pleasers as illogical and emotional, the two most deadly sins in their book. They resent Pleaser people's demands for reassurance and approval and are frightened by their attempts to get close.

Authority reaction to salespeople

Authority prospects distrust and dislike salespeople in general. They regard the entire sales process as an imposition, and do their best to avoid it. They feel they can objectively analyze their own problems and make their own decisions.

Their major question about you is: "What are the facts?" but their unspoken criteria include "Are you logical and objective, or are you a 'typical' salesperson? Will you give me the data I need to make a decision without intruding on my privacy, or will you try to push me into buying something I may not want?"

Most effective approach for Authorities

The guerrilla approach to the Authority is to show how this is the most logical choice, considering the alternatives.

Satisfy their need for control by letting them decide minor matters whenever possible, like the most convenient time to meet or where to have lunch. Give them plenty of time to review proposals and contracts. They have a high capacity for information and detail. Make sure everything is exactly right.

With Authority prospects, the guerrilla must remain detached, logical, and impersonal. Let the facts speak for themselves and keep your personality out of the interaction. Quote third-party authorities. Support your position with figures, percentages, charts, and graphs.

The core of the guerrilla approach

To make sales you must satisfy prospects' needs. There are two types of needs. *Criteria* needs are those your product can satisfy. *Priority* needs are the ones you satisfy through your relationship with the prospect.

Criteria are far more important than priorities. The core of the guerrilla approach to sales is identifying criteria, then demonstrating that your product can satisfy them. You cannot identify or satisfy criteria if you are not sensitive to priorities. Prospects will not answer your questions or listen receptively to your proposals unless they feel comfortable with you.

All prospects want you to care about their welfare, listen to their problems, provide continuing service, act confidently and professionally, and relate to them on their terms.

6
The Budget Stage

Universal money issues

Money! There are few things more difficult to talk about, especially with strangers, and particularly with salespeople. People get weird about money. It seems to have some mystical quality that makes otherwise reasonable people anxious and crabby.

It seems nobody *ever* has enough money. "We can't afford it" is perhaps the objection salespeople most often hear. Money is the very next thing guerrillas discuss once they've found a need. They must confirm that the prospect can afford their product or service. Guerrillas are careful never to present solutions that the prospect can't afford. By dealing with the money issues at Stage Two of the NaB & CaPTuRe selling cycle, guerrillas defuse the "we can't afford it" objection before it turns up.

Priorities and paybacks

Having isolated Needs in Stage One, guerrillas turn the money issue to a tactical advantage by operating in the arena of *priorities* rather than costs and paybacks. If guerrillas can show that a proposed investment in a product or service is a higher *priority* than some other planned expenditure, then the money can be found.

Few of us keep a hundred thousand dollars lying around, but if you were just diagnosed as having a brain tumor and needed an operation, you'd *find* the money. You'd make it a priority.

Getting prospects to tell you how *much* money they have to spend is crucial if you want to sell honestly and professionally. Prospects are often reluctant to reveal how much they have to work with, or even what's allocated in a corporate budget. The reasons are not all that obvious. You may have to deal with the cognitive need in order to stay in control. Ego phase prospects keep their budget close to the vest. As in a poker game, they may feel that showing their hand puts them at some disadvantage.

Prospects may fear paying more than they might otherwise have to, so they hold back this information, waiting for the salesperson to name a more competitive price. We've heard potential home buyers complain about salespeople, "I didn't *want* to tell him how I was going to finance it. I felt it was none of his business. I just wanted him to help me find the *right house*, but he kept asking how I was going to get the money."

A guerrilla would ask something like "Is there a reason why you're hesitant to share this information?" and listen carefully to the answer. Guerrillas need to know a *specific dollar amount* and may need to explain to the prospect that to get the best possible bargain they must be completely frank about finances.

Discovering your prospect's budget

Guerrillas know that people buy *priorities*, not price. If they tell you they're buying strictly on price, they're being less than honest. Priority is based on a combination of factors, including quality, service, warranties, convenience, and even the individual personality phases involved. The most important factor of all is the *pain* you've uncovered in the Need Stage.

The guerrilla never sells on price alone, but justifies the expenditure based on *benefits*. The guerrilla uses this *combination principle*, focusing on the key priorities and criteria, following the progression the prospect will eventually use to justify the purchase to others.

Wish list

You are a professional, and your intent is to do business, and your prospects may not be clear about their own priorities. For example, parents wander up and down the aisles of a toy store at Christmas, clutching a carefully crayoned Santa letter. Their budget is only some vague upper limit.

A guerrilla clerk would start by creating the human bond: "Hi, my name's Janet. You folks look like you could use some help. There are over ten thousand toys here and it's all a bit intimidating."

Now she moves to the Need Stage. "Tell me about your children." She listens carefully, noting their names and ages on a three-by-five card, asking lots of questions about their interests and play habits.

"Of all the things on this list, which do you think your child wants Santa to bring the most?"

"Tell me about the toys they have now."

"Do they have a favorite?"

"Are they artistic or more athletic? Do they play mostly indoors or outdoors?"

"Which ones do you think they would play with most often?"

"Do they have a brother or sister who will share with them?"

"Do you feel it's important that toys have an educational value? If so, here are a couple that would make good choices. Let's start here."

By focusing the conversation on the underlying criteria, the guerrilla helps these parents sort out their conflicting priorities, so they can eventually *justify* spending the money. As every parent knows, we always spend more at the toy store than we budgeted.

Just ask

It's *absolutely* fair to ask your prospects, pointblank, to share their justifications and budgets with you. A guerrilla might ask, "Jim, when you solve this problem, how are you going to tell Mr. Big about your decision?"

You may be able to discern spending priorities from other readily available data. A guerrilla who works in an advertising agency carefully analyzes the annual report of a prospective client, looking for sales data and trends. She also scans other publications, seeking ads for competitive products being launched, and based on her knowledge of what those ads cost, she can extrapolate what the competition is already spending. By applying some simple formulas to these numbers, she can deduce a competitive advertising budget for her client and justify her position based on the company's historic performance.

The budget range finder

When you *do* ask, it's better to do it in easy stages. Your objective is to soften up their defenses by breaching the topic in general terms.

"Off the record," one guerrilla begins, carefully setting his pen down on the table, "what kind of *budget* do you have in mind, in *round numbers?"*

"Somewhere between ten and fifteen thousand dollars."

Once they've told you where the target range is, aim closer and closer to the bull's-eye.

"Closer to ten thousand or closer to fifteen thousand?"

"Closer to fifteen."

"How close?" By asking for progressively precise figures, you make it easier for the prospect to share the specifics. But this still might not give you the whole picture.

What's the problem?

Guerrillas define the budget in terms of a problem that must be solved. A computer software rep might ask, "How much business do you lose because of problems keeping track of your past customers, *approximately?"*

"What might it cost, *ultimately,* if things remained as they are?"

"Can you guess how much it would save if you could solve this problem? Can you give me a *rough estimate?"*

The prospect scratches his head. "Gee, I have no idea."

"Well then, let's take a look."

The standard guerrilla response to "I don't know" is "Guess." You must get a number. Do not be satisfied with a vague "We'll find the money" response.

Finding funding

Often, *spending* the money isn't the issue; it's *finding* the money. Prospects are often unaware of the costs involved, let alone the alternatives for paying. Guerrillas explore their thinking in this area by asking:

"What financial alternatives have you considered?"

Guerrillas may get a straightforward "We'll pay cash" or a direct "We're just looking" or something in-between. If they simply can't afford the purchase, the guerrilla may resort to "Uh-oh, we've got a problem" and exit stage right. But true guerrillas are more tenacious, and more creative. With prospects who look as if they may not have the resources, deal with financial options right up-front. When they realize that they may be able to afford the purchase after all, they will be more forthright about sharing their wants and needs.

Guerrilla financing alternatives

Many companies have discovered the value of extending credit to their customers. Major retailers often generate more profit on the credit card interest than they do on the original merchandise. The guerrilla is careful about introducing the idea of credit. Prospects may be gun-shy about signing up for another credit card. Instead, offer it as an after-thought. . . . "And, of course, if you anticipate being a regular customer, we can open an account for you, and you pay nothing until July."

Bridge to these issues gently, stating them as information rather than as a question. "If you have credit established with another company, or perhaps a major credit card, that would be enough to qualify you for our revolving charge."

Giving customers more time to pay is another tactic. "Our competitors are on COD, but we can give you thirty days to pay, and can extend that an extra thirty days if necessary."

Thinking into the future is a guerrilla concept that has been used by all types of companies, from computer makers to tennis shoe manufacturers marketing to high schools. Because they are establishing user habits at a young age, these students will likely buy these products for the rest of their lives.

Suggest ways for prospects to start using your products and services, even if it's a small start. They may become larger companies in the future, better able to afford enormous orders. There is no need to place a major order right now. A minor order will be just fine, thank you.

Building future sales

Here are more proven, yet little-known guerrilla ideas to help you make many sales in the future:

1. Get them in your club

Companies like Service Merchandise and BizMart have demonstrated the multimillion dollar sales potential of offering memberships to students, seniors, active military, veterans, people with children, government employees, home owners, business owners. The possibilities are endless. Invite them to become members of your Preferred Customer Club. Free. Members get a discount and are notified about sales several days before the general public. Give them a special parking lot or an express check-out aisle.

2. Educate your prospects

Offer low-cost or free workshops and seminars related to your products. Teach potential buyers how they can use a cellular telephone, or how to get the most from a fax machine, satellite dish, or modem. Titles like "Programming Your New VCR" can draw a crowd. Keep the workshops under an hour in length. Serve refreshments. Emphasis must be on real content. This is *not* a sales presentation in disguise. Prospects with a genuine interest and a real need will qualify themselves.

These forums are particularly useful for high-tech items, including the obvious ones like computers and new software and the less obvious ones like microwave ovens and programmable coffee makers. By answering often asked questions in advance, guerillas reduce new-user frustration and pre-empt demand for product support later on.

3. Invite them in

Rent or lease, at little or no cost, your equipment, your office, or your showroom space to prospective clients during your off-hours. Soon these prospects will get spoiled and decide they need equipment of their own. Others will feel more at home there and be more inclined to buy from you.

For certain capital equipment, leasing or renting can be very attractive options to outright buying. Companies can directly deduct the lease payment in the current period, rather than having to depreciate the item over time. There may be investment tax credits, research and development credits, or other tax advantages as well. Because the tax codes change constantly, check with your accountant.

4. Get creative

Creative financing is the norm in the real estate industry. With the current average price of a home in the United States at nearly $150,000 and interest rates often running in double digits, very few first-time buyers can come up with the down payment or meet the monthly mortgage. Yet houses somehow get sold.

The guerrilla uses many of the same creative financing tactics real estate agents use. Help your customers arrange for subleases or time-shares to ease the financial burden for first-time or new start-up clients.

5. Start off small

A guerrilla might suggest that a prospect start off with low-end products and offer a generous trade-in for more high-end future purchases. A real fair-care-share guerrilla might even suggest the client start off small, by buying Volumes I and II, and later add III, IV, and V, rather than buying the whole set at one time. Having two volumes is infinitely better than none at all.

6. Start big

A prospect might be encouraged to make a large purchase in order to take advantage of a volume discount, but take delivery in phases as the payments are made. A butcher who runs a shop in Kentucky often suggests his prospects organize a group of neighbors to split up a side of beef and share the savings.

7. Profit from planned obsolescence

Another guerrilla option is to suggest that prospects sell or rent older, outmoded machinery to smaller start-up competitors and upgrade their own operation to the state-of-the-art product that the guerrilla represents.

8. Take it to the bank

Guerrillas are also ready to assist prospects applying for a bank line of credit to finance their purchases. In the future, these credit lines will become important assets of the prospect's firm. Far-sighted guerrillas arrange these credit lines in advance, offering "preapproved financing" to customers who fit the required profile.[1]

---

[1] For an eye-opening investigation of a whole new world of financing alternatives and a deeper insight into money in America, consult the companion business text *Guerrilla Financing* by Bruce Blechman and Jay Conrad Levinson (Boston: Houghton Mifflin, 1991).

Unique money issues

To help you identify the specific money issues of prospects you are most likely to encounter, we'll look at the classic *Amoral, Ego, Pleaser, Authority,* and *Principle* personalities outlined in chapter three. As in the last chapter, these will be caricatures; very few people possess all the characteristics of the extremes. However, these examples will help you understand how to talk about money with each type.

Amoral prospects

For many of us, money is one of the two or three critical areas of life involving genuine, responsible maturity. Rather than face these issues head-on, some people just temporarily duck and hide, hoping that the issue will solve itself. Should such an Amoral shutdown seem to be occurring with your prospect, it's time to verify that this has happened. You might repeat your last question to the client: "Exactly how did you plan to pay for this?" If you can't get a definite answer, reschedule the appointment. Perhaps you just happen to be meeting at a bad time. Who knows? Your client may have just received a letter from the IRS about last year's tax return. Retreat to base camp.

Ego prospects

Ego prospects are as miserly and selfish about money as they normally are about other aspects of life. Like a new Cadillac in the trailer park, these people's spending priorities can seem out of place. They will only part with their money in order to impress, to appear to be the "best." They're not really interested in how much time a cellular phone will save them, but they are concerned that it be top-of-the-line and better than the one that their colleague bought last week.

When the Ego-phase prospect spends money, you can be certain that the biggest payoff is emotional. Guerrillas need to show that their products and services will help the prospect "win" in the never-ending struggle to succeed and beat everyone else. This can be a factor even when the product is purchased for the good of a large organization and will benefit many others. You must demonstrate *competitiveness.*

Pleaser prospects

Pleasers usually have the least fiscal responsibility. They have the most difficulty with budgets, and even balancing their own checkbook is a real chore. They enjoy buying things, especially for others, and often spend impulsively. Their intent is customarily benevolent, but they may overlook the harsh economic realities in their quest to seem charitable. The guerrilla should show how this purchase will make life more convenient for others, or how much their beneficiary will enjoy it, or show how it will make the world a better place. You must demonstrate *compassion*.

Authority prospects

The Authority likes budgets as much as the Pleaser dreads them. Authority people find comfort and satisfaction in the exactness of dollars and cents. These are people who will spend an hour looking for the missing thirteen cents on the monthly transaction report. They do not buy image or adoration; they are interested only in results. Guerrillas sell them on performance specifications, savings statistics, payback cycles, and attention to the penny detail. You must demonstrate *competence*.

Principle prospects

Mature prospects at the Principle phase are looking for the overall benefit to the firm, to the public, and to themselves, in equal proportions. They want you to give more than you're required to and provide a level of service few other salespeople will. The guerrilla sells them by sharing this broader perspective. You must demonstrate *concern*.

Charlie, a guerrilla who works for Computerland, often pulls out his wholesale price book and shows the figures to his customers. "I just wanted to share this information with you so you can understand how aggressive we are on our pricing. You get the machine you really need, you save your firm a lot of money, and you still have the support of a big-name company like us." That man is a guerrilla.

The bottom line on money

When you know your prospect's need for your product and your prospect's ability to pay, you have completed Stages One and Two of the six-step guerrilla NaB & CaPTuRe Track.

A note of caution: do not go on to Stage Three until you have completed Stage Two. It's a waste to spend any more time with prospects if you can't find some creative way for them to pay. You must clearly establish your prospect's budget and financing options before you go on to the Commitment Stage. The only way to get this information is to ask for it. Remember, the vice president of purchasing isn't necessarily the only one who has the answer.

When talking about money, guerrillas take care to form their questions in a nonthreatening way. They use phrases like "approximately," "in round numbers," "just between you and me," and "off the record."

Guerrillas attack money matters with frankness, openness, and creative options, and help their prospects better understand their own criteria and financial priorities. This financial battle strategy gives them the tactical advantage of knowing that finances will not become a barrier later.

7
The Commitment Stage

Handling objections and summarizing

The third stage in guerrilla selling is to get a commitment to buy. With the completion of this stage of the NaB & CaPTuRe Track, the guerrilla has closed the sale *before* making a presentation. Once the prospect is really committed to solving the problems that have been articulated, all you need to do is tell your story.

By the end of this stage, you should know that your prospect has a need that you can fulfill, has the budget to make the purchase, and has the authority to make some kind of buying decision today. This stage also includes an "NBC Summary" of the three stages covered so far. If your selling cycle requires more than one call, the required buying commitment may simply be the scheduling of another meeting with someone else, arranging for completion of paperwork, or setting up a training session with users.

Handling objections, guerrilla style

As mentioned, the guerrilla must find *at least* one problem or objection that he or she will use to test the intent of the prospect. For the guerrilla, this objection provides an opportunity to turn the control of the conversation back to the prospect.

"So, as I understand you, Jim, you're looking for a high-end office desk with a mahogany finish?"

"Yes, that's right."

"What is it about the mahogany finish that's important to you?"

"Mahogany has such a rich look, especially in an office."

"Well, we've got a problem. It doesn't come in mahogany. Are we finished? Should I go?"

"Well, no, not exactly, how about a dark walnut?"

"No problem, but are you *sure* the dark walnut will create the rich look you wanted?"

"Yes. Perhaps a walnut, or even a dark oak."

"*You're sure?* Okay, let me show you the walnut."

Guerrilla salespeople actually *welcome* objections for several reasons. First, it gives them the opportunity to hand control back to the client, as we've seen.

Next, consider that people will not object unless they're seriously considering your proposition. The worst thing that can possibly happen is that you go through your whole thing, then get to the end and ask, "*What do you think?*" and they say, "Well, no."

Then you say, "*Well, maybe there's something that I didn't explain, or something that you don't understand?*"

"No."

"*No? Well, is there some difficulty with the company? Perhaps there is some problem there?*"

"No."

"*Well, maybe it's me. Did I say something or do something that offended you in some way?*"

"No."

Now you're really stuck! You can't go anywhere from there.

Guerrillas welcome objections with open arms. The first reason is that they are usually *buying signals*. They indicate that you are being taken seriously, but that *the prospect* still has some question or some criteria that hasn't been *fully* answered.

Another reason to welcome objections is that they present an opportunity to *close*. Objections are telling you, essentially, "Well, if you can satisfy this criteria or if you can solve this problem, then we'll go ahead with it." Because most people want to say no before they'll say yes, an objection is one step closer to making the sale. By accepting and dealing with prospect objections before the close, you're giving them a chance to fulfill that psychological need for control of the situation.

Now imagine that you are selling a fine, expensive home, and think about some of the objections you're likely to encounter. All salespeople are likely to run into objections about price. So let's look at several ways to deal with the **"price is too high" objection.**

1. Budget stage before commitment stage

First of all, this objection should have been dealt with in Stage Two, the Budget Stage. However, there are times when prospects insist that they have enough funding for your service, only to find out in the Commitment Stage that their budget somehow shrunk as they "really thought about it."

2. Keep breathing

Remember that objections are buying signals, so the first step is: don't panic. Take a deep breath and refocus your attention on the prospect, then relax. They are actually considering the consequences of this investment and wondering if it's justified. They have, at least mentally, bought the house. At this point, it's not the *house* you need to sell but their ability to pay for it.

3. Clarify

The next step is to clarify the objection, because you really can't answer an objection until you're certain that you know *exactly* what it is. Number one on the list of dumb things that salespeople do is to offer an eloquent answer to the *wrong* objection, leaving prospects feeling pushed and pressured. Instead, clarify the objection by listening carefully and asking questions. You're listening for clues that will reveal their important priorities and criteria.

The better your understanding of the central issues, the easier it will be to answer the objection. Ask questions and probe with phrases like *"Let me make sure I understand exactly what's on your mind. Are you concerned about its resale value?"*

Then *paraphrase* their thinking. Use all the active listening skills you've been learning.

4. Verify

A lot of salespeople tend to jump in with a standard counter-pitch that may be completely inappropriate, instead of responding to the prospects' particular criteria. Guerrilla salespeople never make the mistake of trying to bury the objection in a pile of additional evidence. They never say, "Yes, but it's such a nice house and the pool is so beautiful and it's the best-rated value by the Realty Board," and on and on. If the central issue of the prospects' objection is never addressed, this only serves to strengthen their position and makes them feel pushed and manipulated as well.

You might say, "Well, let me make sure that I understand what you're saying. Do you mean that you can get a less expensive comparable home somewhere else, or do you mean that it's not worth that much to you to live in such a lovely neighborhood; perhaps it's a matter of finances. Can you tell me which it is?"

"Well, I think that I could get a better price *buying direct from an owner.*"

Now, that's a different objection. Price objections can take many forms. You want to make sure that you clarify the objection and hear specifically what the buyer is actually objecting to.

5. Rephrase

It's useful at this point to verify by restating or paraphrasing the objection. This is one of the smartest things you can do, because it lets prospects know that they've been heard and understood, and that it's okay for them to take that position.

"Well, I can understand why you might feel that way. The homes we represent do include a sales commission."

This posture avoids a head-to-head confrontation on the issue and actually strengthens your rapport at that critical time when you need it most. It puts you both on the same side of the fence, looking at the facts. You can also use this opportunity to soften the objection just a little bit by feeding it back in language that is not quite as strong. "There are always a few percentage points included in the price to cover the cost of marketing the house."

Feel, felt, found

A guerrilla way to remember to rephrase is the "feel, felt, found" approach. The general form is "I understand how you *feel.* A lot of people have *felt* that same way. But once they *found* out how beneficial this is, then they feel differently."

For example, the real estate broker might say, "I understand that you *feel* some concern about getting the best possible price on your new home. Every client we've had has *felt* the same way. But when you consider the value of our service and our firm's warranty on the house, and the other financial options we're offering, you'll *find* that it really represents a fair and unbeatable price."

Overcoming objections

Guerrillas are careful not to overreact when they're attacked. They know that most objections are really *questions* in disguise, so they stand their ground and simply answer the issue by providing the appropriate information. But sometimes an objection must be overcome and subdued. Guerrillas hold a black belt in overcoming objections. Like the judo master, they redirect the attack away from themselves and their offering.

1. Content reframing

This tactic is based on changing the *value* of the *content* by putting it in a slightly different context. Just as placing an everyday snapshot in an intricate gold frame elevates the prestige of the subject, the guerrilla can shift people from one point of view to another.

This is accomplished by evoking the *feeling* associated with a particular item or issue, then *swapping* it for a different, more positive feeling.

Let's say that someone is looking at an expensive sports car and says, "I can't see myself driving a car like this; it's kind of racy and frivolous."

First you can respond by saying something like "Well, I certainly couldn't see myself in one that had spoilers or racing stripes on it, or something gaudy like that," in order to acknowledge the objection, then go on to say, "but having the quick acceleration and power that this car has is more than just a frivolous thing; it's really the safety of being able to get out of somebody's way *quickly*. This car handles better and performs better on wet and winding roads, and I certainly don't consider my *safety* to be *frivolous*."

Now look closely at the structure of that response. First, we gave them something to object to that *wasn't* on the car, like the racing stripes. Then we went on to change the *implication* of the *content*. The fact that it's a sports car doesn't mean that it's frivolous; that means it's *safe*.

2. Context reframing

But the guerrilla can also answer objections by altering the *context* of the objection, looking at the same issues from a different vantage point.

Wilson's four-year-old came to him one afternoon and was just beaming! He had, for the first time, put his shoes on all by himself, and he was very excited. And, of course, Wilson, proud papa that he is, looked down at them and said, "That's very nice, Aaron, but you've put them on the wrong feet." Aaron considered his Daddy's objection for a moment, then instantly reframed it by saying, "But, Daddy, these are the only feet I *got!*"

Context reframing is just that: looking at things from a broader perspective. What may seem objectionable at first glance may make more sense in the long run. In dealing with our car buyer who's concerned about the high price, the salesman might say, "Well, this car *definitely* costs a lot more than a Ford or a Chevy or something similar. In fact, it's about *twice* the price on the sticker. But if you think about buying a car in the short run, then it's better to buy a more expensive car because you can finance it over a longer period of time and keep your payments down. You'd actually be spending the same money each month and driving a *much* nicer car. It takes more time before you own it, but in the long run you wind up owning something you can still drive, instead of a pile of junk that has no equity.

"If you think it's cheaper to pay two hundred twenty dollars a month for three years to drive a Ford, as opposed to two-twenty a month for five years for a BMW, look at a five-year-old Ford and compare it with a five-year-old BMW. Check their value and the shape they're in. You'll discover that it's *much* too frivolous and expensive to buy a cheap car. You can't *afford* it."

Remember that your overall motive in reframing the objection is to create a positive emotional experience now that will eventually influence the prospect's buying decision.

3. Isolation

People often buy things in spite of certain shortcomings. Sometimes it's smart to isolate these objections, particularly if you sense that the prospect has really *already* made a decision. Isolating the objection will let you know when the buyer has made the decision and signal you to close. Probe, ask questions, and try to smoke out any additional hidden objections. "Is there anything else that you had any questions or problems with that I can answer?" Sometimes people can get stuck on one objection after another after another after another. Other times they'll raise smoke-screen objections. Maybe they're trying to conceal the fact that, well, they really don't have the authority to make this decision after all, and they've kind of been leading you on. Now it's easier for them to just say no than it is to admit that they've gotten themselves in over their head. So isolate the objection by asking, "Other than that, is there any *other* reason you wouldn't want to go ahead with this?"

4. Just the facts

And then finally, and only then, attempt to answer the objection by presenting additional proof, or taking some other tack — negotiating a price, offering a discount, or offering some additional service to overcome the objection. Very often, as soon as an objection comes up, all salespeople see is a red flag. They think, "Uh-oh, there's a problem here!" And they've heard this objection before, and so they jump in trying to answer it. That's not very smart because people, when their objection is attacked head-on, are going to retrench and become even more defensive.

5. It's just like . . .

Some objections have no obvious answers. Here you might reframe by drawing an analogy, comparing this situation with a similar one. If the prospect complains about the delivery time and there's nothing you can do about it, ask them, "Have you ever been in a situation where you had to wait longer for the right thing, and it wound up being the best decision?" See if there is some other place in their experience where they've been in a similar situation, and use that experience to answer the concern.

Three types of objections

What's the *best* way to handle an objection? The answer is simple: it *depends*. There are several ways that guerrillas answer objections, depending on the type of objection. We'll consider the three most common varieties: the RFI, the Stall, and the Half-Baked Objection.

1. RFI

The most common objection you'll run into is the RFI, or Request for Information, objection. RFIs are actually questions in disguise. Either the prospect has some as yet unanswered criteria or is checking to see if a particular term or item might be negotiable.

Here are some examples:

"Well, I don't like the color."

What is the question the prospect is asking? *Can I get other colors?*

"Gee, we need it sooner than that. We can't wait two weeks for it."
Again, what is the question? *Can you deliver it more quickly?*

"The interest rate is too high." The prospect is really asking, *Do
you think there might be some other way that we can finance this?*

"We can't pay cash for it all in advance like that." *Perhaps there are
other terms available? Are the terms negotiable?*

Handling the RFI

Mentally convert the RFI objection into a question, then answer it.
Stop, think for a second, what is the question that the prospect is asking? Rather than try to handle it as an objection, answer it as if it
were just another question, and it will usually evaporate. *Eighty percent* of all the objections that come up will be Request for Information objections.

Guerrillas *make a written list* of the most common objections and
then convert each one into a question. Place each one on an index
card, together with the answer, and study them until you've memo-
rized them all. This will help you recognize RFI objections when
they come up, and you'll be prepared with an answer.

Guerrillas working on the telephone will write their most common
objections on three-by-five-inch cards and put the answer on the back
side. Then they slip the cards into the plastic sleeves of a flip-up
photo album. The name for each objection shows at the edge of each
card, and when the prospect objects, they simply flip up the right card
and read the appropriate response.

2. The Stall

The second most common objection you'll encounter is the Stall.
"I need to think about it. I never make a decision without sleeping on
it." Or, "I need to discuss this with my (wife, husband, boss, etc.)."
People raise stall objections for one of two reasons: either they really
do not feel comfortable with what they've seen so far, or there's some
hidden condition that they haven't told you about. Maybe they lack
the means to pay or the authority to act.

Handling the Stall

Stall objections are best faced squarely by asking, "If the time were
right, what would you need in order to be able to move ahead with
this?" Prospects who stall are usually motivated by a psychological
need, but it's usually *not* what they're telling you they need, which is
more time.

If a prospect still hesitates, you might summarize by saying, "I'm sure that someone in your position and with your experience can make a decision about this now. Why don't we just go ahead with the paperwork?" Your objective here is to either get them over the hump to the Commitment Stage or elicit their real objection.

You might offer them a special incentive to make an expedient decision: "This is the last one we have in stock," or, "The price is going up next week," or, "I can only offer this concession if we can settle this matter today." If their intentions are genuine, this little extra nudge will be enough to coax them through. If not, then at least you know what you're dealing with.

3. Half-Baked Objections

The third type of objection you'll hear is the Half-Baked Objection. This is usually a far-fetched or petty issue, designed to draw attention away from something else. It's a common negotiating tactic to nit-pick the offer and make the other party's concession seem less valuable. Prospects will sometimes use this tactic to wring a better deal out of a salesperson. Perhaps they want to try to negotiate the price, so they find some minor flaw. These red herring objections are attempts by the prospects to *regain control of the interview for reasons of their own*. It may be because they feel a bit pushed and pressured and just need to exert some influence over the situation.

Vera, a friend of ours, was shopping for a new refrigerator, and asked us to recommend a reputable dealer who would give her a good deal. We made a call to the sales manager of a chain of appliance stores that we had done some training for and asked the manager if he would do us a favor and accommodate a friend. He made an appointment for Vera to come in. After settling rather quickly on the model and color she had in mind, Vera pulled out a copy of *Consumer Reports* and started raving about high markups in the appliance business and how these stores were making entirely too much profit on their poor, unwary consumers. Forty-five minutes later, she finally signed the order, for $38 dollars *more* than the dealer-cost price that the manager had originally offered, on the condition that they deliver the refrigerator.

Later, Vera confided to us that even though the new appliance was exactly what she wanted, she still felt a little bit railroaded, even knowing that everyone had her best interests at heart. Her string of Half-Baked Objections was her way of regaining some control in what she perceived as a pressure situation.

Handling the Half-Baked Objection

You can counter the Half-Baked Objection and still avoid a confrontation by offering your counter-argument as an *opinion*, rather than a fact. You could say, "Well, in *my* opinion, this is the very best value on the market." Or you could say something like, "That may be true, but *I* feel that the price is very reasonable." Since you're describing your *own* feelings and opinions, your position is, in effect, irrefutable.

When to answer an objection

The best time to answer an objection is as soon as possible! Guerrillas often answer objections *before* they're raised, and feel it's better if they raise the objection *themselves*.

Look again at that list you made of your regular objections. There are always a few that you can bet you're going to get. These are the ones that come up over and over again. Now try to incorporate them into your regular presentation. Some salespeople prefer to let sleeping dogs lie, but then you run the risk of them waking up unexpectedly and biting you on the backside.

Pre-emptive strike

When guerrillas raise their own objections, they have a tactical advantage: they *own* the objection, and it's always easier to answer your own objections than it would be to answer someone else's.

Let's say, for example, that people always object to your price because you sell a premium line. It's always better to expect that objection to come up, to take it as your own and bring attention to the issue, then answer it. If you raise the objection, it's your objection and you own it. If prospects raise the objection, then they own it, and they'll feel a psychological responsibility to defend that position. But if you raise the objection and then answer it immediately, they have no investment in its defense.

Anticipate the most common objections: price, terms, delivery, whatever, the ones that come up all the time. Work them out in advance and then incorporate them into your presentation.

Invert the objection

Finally, and this is a guerrilla favorite, you can invert the objection. Just reverse it. If that sounds like a contradiction, it is sort of, but it's probably the single most persuasive way you'll discover to deal with objections, particularly real objections.

A good example is a man who was in one of our classes, a salesman for a local manufacturer of prefabricated, wooden-frame replacement windows. His company's pricing is very competitive because the windows are manufactured locally and don't have to be shipped in from who-knows-where. This man had been calling on a contractor who was putting up a condominium complex at a resort in the mountains and had planned to buy windows from a competitor. The salesman offered a comparable product, and the local price was almost a third less, but he just could not get this man to even consider doing business with him.

A few weeks after the seminar, he told us how he went back to the contractor and used the inverted-objection strategy. First, he started by clearing the air with the prospect; he walked into the developer's office and said, "Listen, I've been calling on you now for six months, trying to get you to buy our windows, and there must be something you feel very strongly about, because I've already shown you how much money you can save. Would you just level with me and share what your real objection is? What is it about our product that is a problem for you?"

"All right," said the contractor, "I don't like your windows because they are hard to open and close."

So the salesman followed the procedure and repeated the objection verbatim: "When you say, 'They're hard to open and close,' what exactly do you mean?"

"I mean, they're hard to open and close. They fit real tight in the frames and it takes a lot of muscle to open and close them. I'm not real happy about that."

"Okay, I can see that, because it's true that our windows do fit tight in the frames and they're a little bit harder to open and close than some of the others. I can see why you would say that."

Then he *isolated* the objection, using the prospect's key criteria. "Other than being hard to open and close, is there any *other* reason why you wouldn't use our product over the competitor's, given the difference in pricing?"

"We spend a lot of money on the finish carpentry in these units, and if you look at the joints, you'll see that we're real sticklers for precision. I just wouldn't feel right putting in some cheap window that didn't fit right."

"Well, I certainly can't argue with that," said the salesman, "and I appreciate your passion for turning out a quality product that's tight and energy efficient. It's only fair that you would want to give your customers the very best." A perfect About-Face.

What he did next was sheer guerrilla. Rather than responding to the charge of being a cheap product, he *reversed* the context: "So I'm sure you understand that the tighter the fit, the *closer* the tolerances have to be. The same is true for our windows and frames. That snug fit is an indication of our precision and quality, and it's *exactly* the reason why you should be using *our* windows, regardless of price.

"While it's true that our windows are slightly harder to open and harder to close, most of the insulation value of a window is lost to infiltration of cold air around the frame. When you consider the insulation value you normally lose to infiltration, our tighter two-pane window is *more* energy efficient than their *three*-pane. It takes a little more effort to open them in the spring, but when you close them for the winter, they close *tight*. If precision is one of your design parameters, you should *definitely* be using our windows."

He walked out of the office with a quarter-million dollar order.

Allow for differences in personalities

Each type of prospect requires a different approach. No matter how persuasive you are, you can't use the same tactics with all prospects. To help you identify the specific issues of prospects you are most likely to encounter, let's look at the *Mind Map* phases again, this time to help you understand how best to talk to the classic *Ego, Pleaser,* and *Authority* personalities when they raise objections.

Ego *prospects*

Make sure you understand their objections before answering. They resent answers that reveal a lack of understanding. Your responses should be forceful and confident, since Ego prospects react positively to clout. However, do not contradict them directly or imply that they don't understand. If they feel that accepting your position would cause them to lose face, they may maintain a position which they know is illogical.

Pleaser *prospects*

Listen carefully and probe gently for hidden objections. Pleaser people hesitate to say things that might offend (such as doubts about you or your company). They are often indecisive and shy of making mistakes, but may be afraid to admit it.

Many of their objections are really requests for reassurance, disguised as questions about the product. Provide assurances about your product, your service, your company, and your concern. If they feel you care about them, they will be less afraid of making mistakes.

Authority *prospects*

Make sure you understand exactly what each objection means, even if you have to ask several questions. Authority people like precision, and they will respect your attempts to get it.

Your answers should be impersonal, factual, and logical. Provide specific evidence whenever possible. These people are particularly impressed by the research of impartial organizations. If you suspect a hidden objection, do not probe too openly. Answer emotional objections indirectly, because these prospects dislike discussing feelings. Ask, "What do you think?" rather than "How do you feel?"

So don't be afraid of objections. Instead, like a hard-core guerrilla, learn to love them. They tell you *why* prospects are not buying. Then you can overcome a prospect's resistance and close the sale. And remember, a true guerrilla always identifies at least one objection to use later to complete the six steps of the NaB & CaPTuRe Track.

The two parts of a buying commitment

Two parts make a buying commitment: the *Who?* and the *When?* The answers the guerrilla seeks are:

1. **You**
2. **Now**

The *Who?* is exposing the internal process and the players involved in purchase decisions. If your prospect has the authority to make the decision, so much the better, but if this purchase requires the approval of another person or a committee, you must find out who and what may be involved.

The second part, the *When?* pinpoints the time that the decision can be made. If it can be made today, wonderful. If not, when does the committee meet again? Can your prospect schedule a committee meeting?

Who?

One guerrilla always begins the *Who?* step with "Jim, can you explain to me exactly how your company makes purchase decisions like this?"

Another begins with "Who else, besides yourself, is involved in making purchase decisions on products?"

Or, "Can you describe for me, in general terms, the buying process at your firm?"

When?

You can open the *When?* by asking, "Jim, assuming I represent a service which will solve the problem you've just explained, within your budget. When do you see your firm using this service?"

Or more directly: "Jim, if I had a product that would fill the need you were telling me about, at the price you just told me, could you make a decision today?"

The guerrilla must get a *specific date*. An answer like "soon" or "as quickly as possible" is not adequate. You want to avoid the "I like to think these things over for a while" objection. If you get a vague answer, suggest a time "soon" when the decision will be made. Something like "When you say 'soon,' do you mean perhaps *today?*" Or respond with, "Since both of us are professionals and work with schedules, can you tell me specifically when you say, 'for a while,' do you mean this afternoon, or that you want to sleep on it overnight, or do you mean someday next week?"

"Fine. *Which* day next week?"

NBC Summary

When you've found at least one objection and have gotten an answer to the *who* and the *when* of the Commitment Stage, you're ready to begin the summary of the first three stages.

Begin with: "So, what I've heard you describe is a real need for . . . and you have $10,000 in your budget to solve this need, and you can make a decision today." Referring to your notes, you describe the criteria uncovered in Stage One that match your product, the budget you heard in Stage Two, and the decision process with a date, like today, uncovered in Stage Three.

Having completed the NBC Summary, you've effectively "closed" this prospect and have subdued the most common buying objections you're most likely to hear when you start to write up the order: no need, no money, no hurry, no authority. With Stage One, you've overcome the "no need" objection. With Stage Two, you've made sure your prospect can afford your product. And with Stage Three, you've made sure you are talking to the right person who can make a buying commitment today.

Congratulations! You've just made the sale. Now all you need to do is describe your product in a way that demonstrates your understanding of the client's priorities. Personalize your presentation to the appropriate personality phase. This is fully discussed in chapter Eight.

After your NBC Summary, your prospect will probably ask to hear more about your product. Great! If you're sure you've heard your prospect's NBC, you're ready to go on to Stage Four. If you haven't, do what you must to hear it.

Home free

In the guerrilla sales track, you now have completed the first three stages. In addition, you've uncovered at least one objection, one problem where your product or service does not exactly fit. You've even offered to end the meeting because of it and you have been asked to continue. Before you go on to Stage Four, the Presentation, you need one more part.

The guerrilla refers to written notes and asks:

"Is there anything that I've overlooked? Are there any other questions you'd like to ask?"

"Yes! When are you going to tell me about your product?"

"Thanks for asking, I'm going to do that right now."

8
The Presentation Stage

Desire and motivation

The key idea in the Presentation Stage, the fourth stage in NaB & CaPTuRe, is that people buy what they *want*, not necessarily what they *need*. Guerrillas know that it's *emotion* that puts the *motion* in motivation.

Naturally, that means your next objective is to create that want, the motivation for the prospect to act on your suggestions, and an active desire to want what they need. They may accept your position, they may agree that you're right, but unless they're willing to *act*, you might as well scrub the mission. You must create an emotional momentum strong enough for them to overcome their natural fear of signing the order.

The NBC Summary has laid the foundation for your personalized presentation. Your job now is to show how your product matches the Need uncovered in Stage One, within the Budget outlined in Stage Two. You also know that your client can make a Stage Three Commitment today. This commitment may be the final order or contract, or it may simply be a confirmation for another meeting leading to the sale.

Organizing the presentation

Your presentation is not a haphazard bunch of ideas and recommendations. It must be clearly structured to cover all your points in logical order. There are three major parts to a guerrilla presentation: the opening, the body, and the summary. All are designed around your prospect's personality.

Gallagher describes the presentation in this way: "First I tell them what I'm going to tell them. Next, I tell them, and then, I tell them what I told them." That is, in the opening, let prospects know what you will discuss, next discuss it in the body of your presentation, then summarize the information.

The opening

The opening lasts approximately **a minute** and should outline your presentation. Your prospects should know where you are headed.

Even if you tell people that you will discuss three points, they may not keep track of all three or see how they fit together. If the points are written down where your prospects can see them, they will feel more comfortable and will follow your presentation better. As all guerrillas know, *points made to the ear and eye are 68 percent more effective* than points made to the ear alone. Show and sell.

For example, a real estate agent's opening statement might be "I'll begin by reviewing your current housing needs. We'll see how much space you need and what kind of extras you're looking for. Finally, I'll discuss the cost of homes of this type."

The body

The body supplies the details. In this case, the agent would discuss individual homes in the area and why they would fill the prospect's "wish list."

Each point is carefully explained, developed, and discussed, organized in a logical progression. To make their presentation more memorable than others, guerrillas discuss the *most important point last*, the second most important *first*, and the least important points in the *middle*.

Guerrillas mark the presentation with clear transitions, so their prospects never get lost. A transition for the real estate presentation might be: "We have seen how this house might work out. Now let's look at another."

The summary

The summary pulls things together and *recommends a specific course of action*. Based on the criteria you've been given, it should be clear by now what the *obvious* choice would be. This is the guerrilla's clear shot. Couch your suggestion as an *opinion* or as a *suggestion*, then ask for confirmation. "In my *opinion*, based on your family's needs and financial considerations, I'd *suggest* that the house on Mapleton Drive *seems* to be the best fit. What do *you* think?"

Your summary also psychologically prepares the prospect for Stage Five of NaB & CaPTuRe, the Transaction Stage. We'll get to that in the next chapter. This stage is the punch line. Your presentation creates the emotional momentum and the desire to buy. You exploit that desire in the Transaction Stage.

Communication styles and the Mind Map

Guerrillas tailor their presentation to fit the style of communication that the prospect has been using. Different prospects have differing personalities, to be sure, but they also have different ways of receiving and processing communication. As you would tune in a radio, you must structure your presentation to properly align with the prospect's way of thinking in order for them to receive your message clearly.

These differences can be summarized in four categories: General/Specific, Options/Procedures, Internal/External, and Proactive/Reactive. We will explain each of these dimensions in depth.

GENERAL . . . . SPECIFIC

Guerrillas adapt their presentation to the appropriate *level of detail* for each prospect, taking into account the prospect's need for explanation and tolerance for specifics. People can fall anywhere along this scale. Some have already made up their mind and would rather not be confused with the facts, while others need large quantities of data and information to make their decision. This spectrum of the *general* to the *specific* is one of the easiest to recognize. *Pay attention to the level of detail that your prospects use* in their conversation and contract or expand your presentation accordingly.

General communication style

People who communicate in the *general* style are most comfortable talking in *sweeping generalities*. They are impatient with minutiae and tend to see things in terms of the big picture, the long term, the overview. *Ego* prospects often fit this description. If conclusion jumping were an Olympic event, these people would be gold medalists. They can be most easily recognized by their monosyllabic answers to questions like:

"How's business?"

"Great!"

"How's your family?"

"Fine."

"How was your vacation?"

"Good."

On a particularly talkative day they might say, "I don't know."

Getting any real information from *generals* can be like pulling teeth. They are *notorious for making assumptions*, because in the absence of hard data they will fill in the gaps based on their general understanding. When outlining their criteria to salespeople, they're often vague and incomplete. Be careful when dealing with *general* prospects, because in their haste to make a deal, they may brush important details aside. Above all, they hate paperwork, so you have to follow through on the particulars yourself, but then guerrillas always do anyway.

Specific communication style

The other extreme of this scale is the *specific*, often seen in *Authority* prospects, who are very precise in their communication and have a very high capacity and *need* for detail. Their conversation is *peppered with specifiers* like place names, references to particular dates and times, percentages, quantities, and distances. They look at the short term, the close-up, and have difficulty understanding the big picture or seeing the overview. Be very careful dealing with *specifics*, because the intent of their communication is often obliterated by all this "detail fog." You have to be absolutely consistent when selling *Authority* prospects because they're alert to the tiniest omission or contradiction.

General vs. specific

You run into problems when you put a *specific* and a *general* together because it's difficult for them to communicate. If their need for detail is exceeded, the more general *Ego* prospect will simply stop listening and daydream about something else. The opposite is true for the more specific *Authority*; unless they have every little bit of information filled in, they have trouble coming to a conclusion. *Pleaser* prospects usually fall somewhere in between. They pay close attention to *personal* details like peoples' names and birthdays, but take a more general approach to impersonal issues like specifications and statistics.

The most effective approach with generals

One of the most frequent fatal mistakes salespeople make is over-loading their prospect with *irrelevant* detail. To communicate with the more general *Ego*, be direct. Do not explain your evidence or your rationale. Go directly to the bottom line, and if they need a more complete explanation, they'll ask for it.

To persuade the *general*, summarize your evidence into capsule form, using charts, graphs, or maps. Pictures help a lot with these people, and *the more concisely you can present your case, the easier it is for them to understand* and accept it. Talk in terms of five-year appreciation rates, community or neighborhood trends, and long-range goals.

To motivate *generals, align your proposition with their long-term plans.* Show them how it fits into the big picture. These people enjoy making decisions, especially big decisions. Give them two or three alternatives and ask them to choose.

The most effective approach with specifics

Specific *Authority* prospects need all the salient facts and then some. To communicate with them, be thorough, complete, and very precise. Explain your reasoning and the evidence that supports it before drawing a conclusion. Show them how your product will perform in exact terms, using dollars, percentages, and dates.

To persuade the *specifics, break your proposition down into incremental commitments.* These people *hate* to make decisions, especially big decisions, so give them a series of little decisions to make instead. You can tie them down on the color, then the quantity, then the shipping method, and finally the delivery date.

To motivate *specifics*, include all the supporting documentation you can get your hands on: computer printouts, brochures, specifications, blueprints, everything. The *Authority* may not read it all, but has an emotional need to feel like he's getting the whole story.

Phase shift

We've studied the work habits of hundreds of professional sales-people, and we've learned that one of the hallmarks of successful guerrillas is *the ability to shift from the general to the specific* in their presentation. They take the general needs of their prospect and apply them to the specific priorities and criteria that are most relevant. Then they translate them into general terms a lay prospect can understand.

Because the guerrilla's communication fits them like an old shoe, prospects are comfortable making the required decisions and commitments.

OPTIONS . . . . PROCEDURES

Another dimension the guerrilla can consider is the *need for order and structure*. Think in terms of a scale with *options* at one end and *procedures* at the other. Keep in mind that a person can fall anywhere along this scale, and their position on one scale may be completely unrelated to their position on the other scales.

Options-style communication

You can recognize the *options* client as soon as you walk into the prospect's office. This is the person who has nine file folders open on the desk, is talking on the telephone, writing a letter, and carrying on a conversation with you, all at the same time! These folks are multimodal and are often good at handling multiple demands and simultaneous tasks. They organize their work as a set of *alternatives*, and if they've got five things on their list of things-to-do-today, they may start with item number three and work on that for a while, then jump to item one, make a dent in that, then go to number five, and so on. They are notorious for starting projects and not finishing, so you have to follow up carefully on any commitments they make. *Ego* and *Pleaser* people most often exhibit this pattern.

Procedural-style communication

The *procedural* prospects, on the other hand, organize tasks as a check list, to be accomplished sequentially, step-by-step. They'll start with item number one and work on it till it's finished. Then and only then will they go on to number two, and if they get interrupted in the middle of their procedure, they have to start all over again. This is *very* stressful. Perhaps you know or have worked with someone like this. They'll say things like "Look, I can only do one thing at a time!"

The *procedural* style of communication can be either a resource or a liability, depending on the demands of the situation. A receptionist who is highly procedural will be resentful if she's typing a letter and your entrance interrupts her routine. She loses her place and has to start over, and it drives her crazy. So the guerrilla has to learn to stand quietly and watch until she stops to reach for a document or otherwise interrupts her procedure. Then the guerrilla can approach her with a question.

The most effective approach with options

Similarly, guerrillas adapt the presentation to follow the organizational strategy of the prospect. To communicate with the *options* prospect, be flexible. Nothing turns the *options* prospect off quicker than a canned pitch. Be prepared to follow them on a roller coaster ride up, down, and around the issues. A carefully planned presentation is of *particular* value here, even if it isn't followed sequentially, because like a road map, it helps you get the conversation back on course.

The *Pleaser* is moderately flexible in an effort to gain acceptance, while the *Principle* prospect is genuinely open to alternative points of view. These prospects may interrupt with questions or comments, and you must give them somewhat of a free reign in directing the conversation.

To persuade the *options* prospect, spell out several available alternatives, showing how *your* suggestion is the *best* available option.

Guerrillas motivate *options* prospects by giving them a set of alternatives and asking them to make a choice. Be careful not to give them *too many* possibilities, particularly if they are also *general*. You may launch them into paralysis by analysis.

The most effective approach for procedurals

Authority prospects are often highly procedural. They follow the known course and are not pioneers. There is one right way to do everything: *their way,* and any deviation violates their need for order and correctness. To communicate with these people, you must follow your carefully prepared presentation step-by-step. If you digress, use an "as I was saying, . . ." transition to get back into your outline. It helps if you give them a copy of your notes. If you can present from an outline, checking off each issue as you cover it, so much the better. This taking-them-by-the-hand approach makes it possible for them to follow your train of thought.

To persuade the *procedural*, structure your case as the *only* logical way to proceed, given the evidence. If you can lead the *Authority* to a logical conclusion, based on the facts, it's easy for them to go along with your deal. Also keep in mind that procedural people *resist change,* so talk in terms of "progression," "evolution," and "improvement," rather than "new," "revolutionary," or "breakthrough."

To motivate the *procedural*, give them a demonstration or show before-and-after pictures. If they follow some routine, find out what it is. If they reorder on a regular schedule, make sure you're in touch with them on *exactly* the same day each month to take their order. Whatever you do, be *consistent*.

INTERNAL . . . . EXTERNAL

Another dimension that you can listen for is *motivational frame of reference*. Prospects differ in their strategies to maintain their motivation, and one of the most important things to note is the *locus of the feedback they depend on for their decisions*. Do they look for feedback internally or externally? Finding out will help you communicate in a way that builds powerful motivation.

The basic question to ask the prospect is "How do you know when what you are doing is working?" or "How do you know when what you have bought is doing a good job for you?" For example, a guerrilla might ask her house-hunting prospects, "Based on your experience, how do you know when you've found the right house?"

External frame of reference

Externally motivated prospects tend to respond with something like, "I want a place where I don't have to be embarrassed if clients come to visit." Or they might say something like, "The view is really important, and has to be impressive, maybe on a lake or on a golf course."

These prospects are fixing their frame of reference *externally*, on the *outside* world, on what others might say or feel. The impression the house will make is an important consideration for externally motivated buyers. They base their decision on factors found in the *environment*.

Authority, Pleaser, and *Ego* prospects tend to be progressively more *external*, respectively. *Authorities* are concerned with whether a decision is "right," according to their internal rules and outside experts; *Pleasers* are concerned with whether it will make other people happy; and *Egos* are concerned with whether it will make them look good.

Internal frame of reference

Internally motivated people test values and standards *within their own being*, by their sense of comfort, their gut reaction, their conscience, their intuition and judgment. They base their decisions on factors inside themselves, a vision, a feeling, or a voice inside their head.

The internally motivated prospect might respond to the same question by saying, "You just know when it's right. You get a feeling when you first walk in. Is it cozy? Is it solid? If I'm going to spend five or ten years in a house, it has to be comfortable." This prospect might be interested in the same house as the externally motivated buyer, but for very *different* reasons. The relationship with the agent will be different as well. *Principle, Responsible,* and *Universal* phases tend to be progressively more internal. *Principles* are concerned with whether it's fair-care-share; *Responsibles* are concerned with whether it will achieve their personal goals; and *Universals* are concerned with how it fits their vision of the world.

Most effective approach for externals

This is important, because people who are externally motivated, the *Authority,* the *Pleaser,* and particularly the *Ego,* are, in fact, *dependent* on information input, statistics, and testimonials; they have to have that stuff in order to make a decision. They want you to tell about your proposal, make suggestions, even prescribe a particular course of action. They expect you to provide third-party references, demonstrations, recommendations, and more.

Presenting to an externally motivated prospect, the agent could make comments like "This house has the biggest trees on the block" and "I can just see your friends will be green with envy when you move in." The externally motivated want input and feedback. They want the agent to say, "I think this is *just* the place for you." To sell the *external,* tell your story and offer third-party testimonials.

Most effective approach for internals

Internally motivated prospects make decisions independent of what's going on in the real world. These people really don't care what you think (or anyone else, for that matter). You have to ask about *their* opinions, feelings, and values. "What do you think of this view?" or "Can you imagine curling up in front of this fireplace with a good book?"

Use questions to help them access their internal judgment, because that's the scale they'll use for weighing the evidence. Their ears believe most what their own mouth says. It makes them uneasy if you try to load them up with rave reviews. Not only do they ignore it, they resent it.

The guerrilla accesses their internal motivational mechanism by saying, "Well, I'm sure that *you* understand your family's needs better than I do, and I'm really dependent on your feedback as we tour different properties. I'd like to be your realtor, but ultimately you have to live with your decision."

Motivation and the Mind Map

Figure 8.1 demonstrates where the various phases of the Mind Map fall on the internal/external scale. Guerrillas will keep these differences in mind when concluding their presentation.

INTERNAL . . . . EXTERNAL

Universal   Responsible   Principle   Authority   Pleaser   Ego

---

Fig. 8.1

Guerrilla selling also means maintaining an awareness of your *own* motivational style. Externally motivated salespeople often mistake a rejection of their *product* for a rejection of *them* personally. They are overly focused on external evidence. Internally motivated salespeople think they're doing great when they've actually missed the boat with their prospect. They're preoccupied with their own thoughts and judgments. *Pleaser* and, particularly, *Ego* salespeople need regular praise, recognition, and feedback about their work. When their performance is substandard, they need to be reminded what the expectations and rules are. They strive to win contests and awards. They interpret information as instructions. They want participation and input from others on their work.

Authority salespeople are somewhat external and somewhat internal. They will let the weekly sales figures speak for themselves when it comes to recognition. They require careful coaching in the beginning, but once they decide that they know the rules, they become self-managing. After a careful training period, they need to be given a free hand, with only periodic checkups. They do not want to be told how they're doing; for them, you're just restating the obvious. They are not as interested in recognition or awards, but they will work very hard to meet standards and goals, particularly those they've set for themselves.

Which are you? Are you motivated by what others say or think or by your own gut feeling? Guerrilla selling means adapting to the motivational needs of your prospects, and striving to appreciate both their feelings and intuition, as well as the external feedback on the tote board. Over-reliance on one at the expense of the other can lead to disaster.

Initiative in your prospects

Another thing to watch for is your prospects' level of initiative. Do they take the initiative to make things happen, or do they wait for others to get things started?

PROACTIVE . . . . REACTIVE

Proactive prospects like to be in control and make things happen. They tend to jump in with both feet. They have a bias for experimentation over analysis, and tend to *act first and ask questions later*. *Reactive* prospects prefer for someone else to do the driving and take them along for the ride. They have a bias for analysis over experimentation, and tend to *ask questions* relentlessly rather than *act*. *Principle*-phase prospects are often highly proactive, and *Ego* prospects often fit this description in excess. *Authority* prospects are more reactive, while *Pleaser* prospects may be reactive in the extreme.

The proactive style

The *proactive* prospect wants to take the lead, to be in control, and in severe cases, may resist the initiative of others, including you. In selling, follow their lead and *treat everything as if it were their idea*. These people are go-getters. Inaction makes them uncomfortable. If you promise to send a brochure or catalog, get it out the same day, and *expedite everything*. They prefer to try your product out, but if it doesn't work the way they expect it to the first time, that's enough. They're ready to deal with someone else.

With proactives, any actions on your part will be well received. They respect people of like mind and are happy to push things along. They make great allies within an organization because they tend to ferret out any resistance to a project they've started. Be careful if you meet one of these who is also *internal*. He may make commitments he can't keep.

The reactive style

At the other end of the scale we have the *reactives*. These prospects are not motivated to start things, but instead rely on the initiative of others, so take the lead by making suggestions and recommendations. Be prepared to sell the reactive *Authority* prospects with facts, figures, and test results, and take the initiative to offer samples, do a trial run, or in some other way get the ball rolling. *Pleasers* are afraid to rock the boat; they prefer the status quo and may be resistant to change. With the *Pleaser*, who tends to respond to the opinions and recommendations of others, be prepared to present testimonials and references, and get friends, boss, or spouse involved.

Reactives may perceive your initiative as being pushy, but they will react to it, either positively or negatively. They require constant attention, checking back, and prodding along, or the momentum of the sale will be lost.

Figure 8.2 shows how the most frequently encountered personalities fall on the proactive/reactive scale.

PROACTIVE . . . . REACTIVE
Ego   Principle   Authority   Pleaser

Fig. 8.2

Constellations of styles

Guerrillas carefully analyze constellations of needs when developing their presentations. Immediately after the initial meeting, the guerrilla may zip off a quick deal memo to the *Principle*-phase CEO, who is *internal*, *general*, and *proactive*.

Then the guerrilla takes the time to write a carefully worded cost/benefit analysis for the *Authority*-phase production manager of the same company, who is *externally* motivated, *specific*, and *reactive*. A thank-you card goes to the *Pleaser*-phase division manager, who is *specific*, *externally* motivated, and *reactive*, itemizing all the little things done to facilitate the presentation. Another short note is sent to the *Ego*-phase sales manager, who is *general*, *proactive*, and *externally* motivated, congratulating him on the success of his idea. In this way, guerrillas cultivate a favorable motivational environment for their product or service. It's hard work, but it's remarkably effective.

Tie everything to the prospects' priorities

The first three stages (NBC) give you insight into prospects' priorities and criteria, and you've been listening carefully to diagnose their preferred patterns of communication. Now the guerrilla uses that information to match the presentation to the prospect.

If the prospects are considering alternative solutions, show how your service or product is superior, not in a general sense, but as a solution to their particular want or need. Many salespeople ignore competition. They talk only about their own products, leaving the comparison to the prospect. Guerrillas know that if the prospect makes the comparison, it will be less favorable than if they make the comparison themselves. Guerrillas invite comparison, because they've researched the competitors thoroughly. State exactly how your product does a better job, but make sure that you do not appear to be knocking the competition. That tactic offends some prospects. A guerrilla tactic is to talk up the competitor, then show how your own product is *superior*. A guerrilla banker might begin by reviewing with a prospective loan applicant the *normal* loan process and various *standard* fees and then how *his* bank offers better service at more competitive rates. This information could be verified by a competent third-party source like *Consumer Reports*.

When you directly relate your product or service to your customer's wants and needs and show how it's superior to the competition's, your job becomes much easier. When prospects understand why they should buy, they also will have more confidence in you. They recognize that you are not just making a canned presentation or "letting the product speak for itself." You are working with them to solve their problems. Guerrillas are world class problem solvers.

Features, advantages, benefits, and pain

Prospects are much less interested in your product than in how it can relieve them of some want, need, or *pain* they're experiencing. They want to know what it can do for them; how it will eliminate some discomfort. They care about its benefit, not its features.

The difference

A *feature* is what it *is*, an objective and observable characteristic; it's always the same, regardless of whether one buys or not. For example, features of a resort hotel might include two hundred rooms, a full-service restaurant, and two heated pools with adjoining spas.

An *advantage* is what the feature *does*, the function that it performs.

The heated pools provide a place where guests can exercise, socialize, and relax, that's what they *do*. But that's not the end of the story.

A *benefit* is the payoff of the advantage, or the *value* a feature provides to the prospect. Year round use means that guests can relax or exercise *any time they want to*. Conventions can be scheduled any time of the year, and attendees will be more relaxed and more receptive to the new ideas they will hear. Benefits solve problems; benefits relieve pain.

Benefits are defined by the *prospects'* needs. The same service will offer different benefits to prospects with different priorities and criteria. For the physical fitness buff, the heated pool may mean exercise. The couch potato types may like the relaxation aspect of a heated pool and spa.

These benefits will be more appealing to the prospect if you dramatize them.

"Sure it costs us a bit more to heat our pools year round, but after a full day of conference activity, you know how great it feels to swim a few laps and lounge in a warm spa under the stars."

But what about intangibles?

As with all products and services, even intangibles have features, advantages, and benefits. For example, the features of a life insurance policy might include a double indemnity clause for accidental death, a waiver of premium, and common carrier triple indemnity.

An advantage is what the feature does, the function that it performs. The double indemnity *pays twice the face amount* of the policy should the death be from other than "natural causes." Waiver of premium means if the insured is unable to perform his or her normal job because of an accident or illness, *the monthly payments will be waived*. Triple indemnity means the policy will *pay three times the face amount* if the insured's death occurs on a public bus, boat, train, or plane.

Remember, though, that a benefit is *the value of the advantage to the prospect*. Waiver of premium means the owner doesn't have to *worry* about keeping the insurance in force if there's an accident or a prolonged illness.

Because the same product or service with the same features will offer *different* benefits to different prospects, the guerrilla adapts the presentation to cover *selected features* that offer *advantages* that are relevant to this prospect's criteria and *benefits* that satisfy his priorities.

"You know how awful it would be if a drunk driver hit you on the freeway and you were laid up for a month or so. One of the things you wouldn't want to worry about is your life insurance payment. That's what waiver of premium means."

Get it in their head

The guerrilla paints a word picture of the prospect *using* the product, *benefiting* from it, and *enjoying* it. It's essential that you involve your prospect's senses and imagination. By evoking feelings in a particular direction, you create a favorable motivational climate for your proposal.

Future pacing

The guerrilla achieves this by using a transition that takes the prospect across time frames. For instance, right now, as you read this far into the book, you've absorbed a lot of information, and you may find that you experience some difficulty piecing it all together and integrating it.

However, you'll find that when you go into the field tomorrow or back to your office, situations described in this book will come up, and things will suddenly connect for you. Almost intuitively, you'll find yourself applying guerrilla skills in your interactions with people, and you won't even have to try. You'll be surprised to find it happening for you automatically, because you now have an enhanced awareness of peoples' needs, and you'll feel more confident and better prepared to respond in appropriate ways.

Now, stop reading ahead and look again at the last paragraph. Read it carefully. This is an example of a transition across time. It provides a glimpse into your future, and it's a technique that we've used throughout this book to maintain your interest and to motivate you to continue. *Employing this tactic will generate an impressive increase in your income.*

The first step is to set the context in what you're experiencing right *now*, and then *shift* the context into the future using word pictures. Remember that before you can move your prospect to a new perspective, you must start with them within their current perspective. The guerrilla starts out with the prospects in the here-and-now, and then gently eases them forward into the future.

Finally, guerrillas attach a particular *feeling* to the experience they'd like the prospect to feel. It's this feeling that will clinch the decision, so the guerrilla will attach a feeling that's positive and supportive of the proposition.

Three ways to create motivation

There are three ways you can use this tactic to connect positive feelings to your proposal, or to defuse negative feelings that might obstruct the sale.

1. Confront the monster

Read carefully how this guerrilla real estate agent eliminates indecision by referring to the doubt the prospect is probably experiencing:

"Buying a house is a big decision, and it's real scary for a lot of people. It's probably the single largest investment they'll ever make. And you're probably asking yourself, 'Gee, am I sure about this? Is this really the right house?' And of course you're *not* sure, and you might not be able to answer that question today. But I'll tell you what; six months after you've moved into this place, and you've got all your furniture in here, and you've trimmed up the lawn and painted the eaves, this house is going to be gorgeous. You'll feel very, very proud. You've added your own touches and made it your home. That's when you'll know that you've made the right choice."

The Presentation Stage moves the prospect from the *present* into the *future* through a mental experience of living in the house and feeling good about it as a result. The guerrilla painted a beautiful, rosy picture, then put the prospects into it. This gives them the benefit of knowing what it will look, sound, and feel like, so they can consider those factors in their decision right now.

2. Share personal experience

The second way to apply this tactic is to use your *own* experience to demonstrate the outcome you're going for:

"When we bought our first home, I remember how difficult it was to make the decision, and how uncertain we felt because the house we moved into seemed to have a lot of things wrong with it at first. But in just a few weeks, it felt like home sweet home. Even now that we live in a much larger house in a much nicer neighborhood, I still get nostalgic for that little place on 18th Street."

In this case, you're using an example of how *you* felt under similar circumstances to draw a parallel.

3. Third-party testimonial

The third, and by far the most common variation, is to use a third-party example: "A couple that I worked with a few years ago was absolutely *certain* that they were making a big mistake. The house and the yard were somewhat larger than they really wanted, and it came with payments to match. But right after moving in, they discovered that they were expecting a baby! Now their little girl has her own bedroom, a sunny playroom, and a nice, safe fenced yard. Even though it was a financial stretch, they were really glad they hadn't settled for less."

Notice how the salesperson used descriptive phrases like "big mistake" and "absolutely certain" to acknowledge the prospects' feelings of uncertainty, then shifted to create positive feelings with "sunny playroom," "safe fenced yard," and "glad that they hadn't settled for less." The guerrilla associates these positive feelings with the specific features of this house to motivate the prospect to buy now.

Even when they really want to buy, prospects will have a few butterflies when the time comes to write up the paperwork. This tactical communication respects the emotional uncertainty that your prospects are going through in their struggle to make a decision, and helps overcome any emotional resistance they might have. This approach gives them the emotional momentum to carry through the Transaction and Reward Stages.

By the end of this stage, the prospect will want to ask you to write up the order. The guerrilla creates such a strong desire that at the end of the Presentation Stage, clients will get out their checkbooks and start writing.

KISS = Keep It Short and Simple

Remember, your goal isn't to tell the prospect all you know; it is to get the order. A guerrilla can be specific without going into long stories or giving excessive detail. Many salespeople go into excessive detail because they're afraid prospects will not understand. The shorter and simpler your presentation is, the better your chances for the sale. By concentrating the presentation *exclusively* on the criteria and benefits outlined by the prospect as priorities, the guerrilla makes the job easier for everyone.

Prospects rarely get upset if a presentation is shorter than they expect. You may believe you have to cover every point, but most prospects just want the highlights. If prospects want to continue past the alloted time, remind them that your time is up, but you will be glad to continue if they *insist*. This maintains the integrity of the time frame you promised in the beginning.

Avoid buzz words

A sure way to blow the sale is to make the prospects feel stupid by using terms they may not understand. Nearly all prospects are irritated and confused by jargon. You may think that using the buzz words of your field demonstrates your knowledge and sophistication. Usually it just kills the prospects' enthusiasm. Stay with what the late advertising great Leo Burnett termed "shirt-sleeve English."

Illustrate with stories and props

With the possible exception of the *Authority*, abstractions and statistics do not move people. Stories, pictures, and examples do. Selling a home security system, a guerrilla would not cite a host of crime statistics. Guerrillas would ask their prospects to imagine a burglar breaking in and hear their children screaming.

A guerrilla who sells houses in Orange County measures her prospects' furniture, then makes life-size cardboard cutouts of each piece. When the couple responds positively to a house she's showing, she pulls out the cutouts and begins laying them out on the floor "just to see how things will fit." She knows she's sold the house when they have agreed on the best location for the TV.

Unfortunately, visual aids are often neglected because salespeople do not know how to use them effectively. Do not rely on them to sell your product or service. Use them only *after* your NBC Summary. The more senses you can appeal to, the more effective your presentation will be. Let prospects see it, touch it, hold it, or sit on it. If at all possible, let them pick it up and feel its weight.

End with a bang

Your summary should be dramatic and memorable. Your entire presentation should build toward the summary in exactly the same way a good play builds toward the final curtain. This is when your prospects' desire is at its peak and they are most likely to order.

Adjust to prospects' personalities

By now, you should have a very clear idea which phase of the Mind Map your prospect is operating from. Now you can modify your presentation style to tune in to their priorities and criteria based on their personality.

To help you identify the specific presentation issues of prospects you are most likely to encounter, we will focus on the most common personalities and look at how you might adapt to the *Ego*, *Pleaser*, and *Authority* personalities. Naturally, you wouldn't have gotten this far with shut-down *Amoral* types, and with *Principle* prospects just tell your story; they'll understand that you are fair-care-share.

Ego *prospects*

Egos tend to be impatient and do not enjoy listening to long presentations. Be brief, well organized, and avoid detail. Never stretch the truth with them. Exaggerations will increase their natural skepticism and give them a chance to attack you. Remember that for the Ego, everything is a contest, so don't become flustered if you're attacked.

Don't try to anticipate and respond to every possible objection. That would make your presentation too long. When you are talking, you are in control, which makes the Ego uncomfortable. So keep it short.

It's important that you maintain your clout with Ego prospects. They may interrupt frequently with objections or questions. Do not fight the interruptions or evade their points, but do stay firmly in control of the presentation. Reinforce their self-esteem by acknowledging their right to interrupt by saying, "That's a good question," or, "I'm really glad you brought that up." Then respond directly. If you lose control, they lose confidence in you.

Pleaser *prospects*

Pleasers respond well to authority as long as it's combined with warmth and personal concern. Show your interest in an authoritative, but not particularly forceful manner. Relax and share control. Encourage a dialogue. If they digress, gently bring them back on track.

Authority *prospects*

Authority people like details and want specific evidence to support your points. Your presentation should be detailed, impersonal, factual, and somewhat longer than with Egos and Pleasers. Prepare fact sheets or handouts in advance. Put the bulk of the details and evidence in the handouts and check them carefully for accuracy. Authority prospects read material very carefully and are intolerant of errors. They are likely to ask questions about the handouts, so make sure you understand every point. If they pump you on a minor point and you do not respond satisfactorily, it may destroy your credibility and the sale. If you don't know the answer, say so and tell them that you'll make a phone call right now to get the explanation they need.

Your *personality*

Finally, adjust your presentation to take advantage of your own personality. If you tend to be an Ego personality, exploit your natural power, but do not overwhelm prospects. If you are primarily a Pleaser salesperson, use your natural warmth and sensitivity, but make sure your presentations are forceful and well organized. If you tend to operate as an Authority, build on your diagnostic and organizational strengths, but shorten your presentations, appeal to feelings, and communicate more warmth.

Guerrillas always ask themselves: *Is what I am about to do or say fair for all concerned? Will it communicate that I sincerely care? Will it be apparent that I am always going to give more than the competition?* This bit of internal questioning will safeguard you as a *Principled* salesperson.

Remember, *everything* you do communicates a message. By targeting the communication needs of your prospects and responding in a way that fits their wants and needs, you make your proposal easy for them to understand, accept, and act upon. That's the hallmark of a guerrilla salesperson.

Okay, now you've reached the end of your personalized presentation and you've shown how your product matches your client's criteria and priorities. It's time to shift your posture and take a deep breath as you move into the Fifth Stage of NaB & CaPTuRe.

9
The Transaction Stage

"Something's bothering me ..."

As you begin the Fifth Stage of NaB & CaPTuRe, clients sometimes stiffen. "Uh-oh, here comes the order blank." Many customers dread this moment; they feel as though they're losing control even if they really need the product and can afford it. Understanding this, guerrillas move deftly into this new stage, ending the Presentation Stage with something like:

"Well, that about sums it up. Do you have any questions?" The prospect now feels a little more relaxed.

"No, not really."

"Is there anything else you'd like me to take care of?"

"Not really."

"What do you see as the next step?"

"Well, don't you have to write up an order?"

"Do you *want* me to write up the order?"

"Well, yes. I do."

Music to the guerrilla's ears! Your prospect is now a client, and this new client just asked you to write up the order! With that, the guerrilla fills out the order form, writes up a contract, or prepares the financial paperwork. Now the guerrilla hands the form to his new client for his or her approval.

As the new client is about to sign, beginning the Transaction Stage, the guerrilla softly interrupts:

"You know, something's still bothering me, remember back there, when you said you wanted mahogany? Are you *sure* walnut is going to be okay?"

What the guerrilla wants to hear is something like "Yes. In fact, walnut is really going to be much better. It will be cheaper than mahogany and fit in better with the rest of the office decor."

"Are you really sure?"

"Yes."

To begin the Transaction Stage, a guerrilla will recall at least one problem or objection and stress concern about it. You must ask again if the concern is going to be a problem. In so doing you are again turning control over to your client, and you're preventing buyer's remorse.

Buyer's remorse usually occurs a day or two after an order is written up. The new customer may get nervous about the purchase and call, stating he or she really needs the furniture in mahogany. By capping the issue now, the guerrilla pre-empts this potential problem.

This technique can be used almost anywhere in the six-stage guerrilla selling track. It can be used anytime the guerrilla senses the prospect may feel a loss of control. The guerrilla begins with "Something's bothering me , . . ."

But if they don't ask, close

People try to put off making decisions, especially big decisions. A few years back a study was conducted to learn Americans' attitudes about decision making. A huge percent of the people said that they *hated* to make decisions, even simple decisions like "What would you like for breakfast, dear?"

Ever invite a friend to lunch and find out he's got decidophobia?

"Hey, let's go out to lunch!"

"Oh, all right, where do you want to go?"

"I don't know, where do you want to go?"

"Well, you decide."

"No, you decide."

People just don't want to make decisions, and the bigger the decision, the more they hate to make it. That's why restaurants have daily specials. It's for all those folks who can't deal with a whole menu full of options.

So what if the prospect doesn't ask you to write up an order? You must flex your mental muscles and ask for it directly. This is traditionally called "closing," but guerrillas know that if the sale has not already been made, a great close won't save the day. There is an enormous difference between wanting and buying. A great close will not result in an order unless the prospect wants, needs, and can afford your product or service. The close is the push that some prospects need to take the final initiative. You know you've done everything *right* when the *prospect* closes the sale for you.

When to close

Guerrillas recognize *when* to close and know that closing is best done on *choices, challenges,* and *changes*.

Close anytime there is a *choice* or decision to be made, and that's more often than you might think. Someone buying a car has to consider the make, the model, the color, the special equipment, the price, and ultimately the dealer. The car buyer will make over 400 individual choices before finally driving away. Close early and often, especially on little things. Because people hate making big decisions, guerrillas close on the small ones.

Always close after answering a *challenge* or objection. A prospect who accepts your answer will be receptive to making a commitment. Guerrillas automatically finish their explanation with a closing question like "Did I answer your question adequately?" or "Is that clear now?" Check and make sure that the objection has been answered to the prospect's satisfaction.

Also close anytime there are *changes* in your prospects' body language or changes in their answers that could be interpreted as buying signals.

Timing your transactions

Timing is critical. Guerrillas take a hide-in-the-trees-and wait-until-they-get-a-clear-shot approach to closing. They watch for signals that the prospect is ready to make a decision. They do not close when prospects seem disinterested, confused, or otherwise not ready to act. Closing at the wrong time can create a win-lose confrontation and turn off an otherwise interested prospect. For example, a prospect has shown considerable interest, but has just said, "I don't understand how that feature works." Do not risk killing the sale by attempting to close now. Instead say, "If you like that particular model, I'll be happy to explain it."

Indications of buying readiness are known as "buying signals." Anything the prospect says or does that tells you they're ready can be interpreted as a buying signal. A real estate agent in one of our workshops once explained, "I know they've bought the house when they start talking about which kid gets which bedroom."

Sometimes prospects are not as subtle. They might ask, "Can I write a check?" This is a buying signal. "Do you accept American Express?"

This, too, is a buying signal. But guerrillas know that buying signals may be *indirect* as well. "Do you deliver?" That's a buying signal. "Do you have this in red?" That's a buying signal. "What do you think they'll say in Accounting?" That, too, is a buying signal. Although it doesn't necessarily bring with it a commitment, the prospect is definitely giving you some encouragement. "Can I get this installed?" or "What's the warranty?" or "Can I exchange it if it doesn't work?" or any similar question usually means they've already made a decision.

Keeping your eyes wide open

Most buying signals are subtle, and you have to pay close attention or you'll miss them. Perhaps the prospect begins taking notes or confers with a colleague or spouse about a particular item. In a retail store, a sharp clerk can decipher the briefest comment about a color, or an admiring glance at a rack at the other end of the aisle. Changes in voice tone are often important buying signals. If calm matter-of-factness begins to turn to excitement, or if nervous chattering begins to settle down and become more businesslike, you've got yourself some buying signals.

Crossed arms that uncross, leaning forward in a chair, a still pencil that begins tapping are all buying signals. Particular cues are a relaxing of the face around the eyes and mouth, folding the hands in the lap or behind the head, or uncrossing the legs. These are signals that the buyer's resistance is melting into acceptance. If you have any doubts, watch for more. Buying signals usually come packaged together.

Learn to close early

If you do not close in the Transaction Stage, you'll probably never get the sale. All salespeople have had the experience of nearly closing the sale, returning confidently to take the order, then running into a brick wall. When this happens, they usually conclude that prospects are just irresponsible jerks.

There is nothing strange or unusual about the prospect's behavior. You probably act the same way yourself. Think back to the big decisions in your life such as getting married, changing jobs, or buying a house. You didn't just analyze the facts and make a decision. You were *scared*. You worried and discussed it repeatedly and kept putting off making the big commitment. That is how prospects feel, even if the decision is a small one. You know that people do not like to make commitments. We are all afraid of making mistakes, and we have been told hundreds of times: "Never sign anything."

A guerrilla we know uses action close at the *beginning* of his presentation of a new stereo system by asking the prospect, "How far from the amplifier will you be putting the loudspeakers?" Based on the prospect's answer, he goes to the service counter, measures off a length of wire, *cuts it*, ties it in a bundle, and hands it to the prospect. Now she's sitting there, holding the *first* component of the new stereo that she's about to buy. Very effective. Very guerrilla.

Overcoming fear of closing

Most people want consistency in their ideas and actions. If they conflict, people feel uncomfortable and change either their ideas or their actions until they become consistent. You know you should close more often, but each time you risk rejection and failure. To avoid a potentially painful situation, you may not close as often as you should.

Some salespeople are so afraid of rejection and failure that they won't ask for the order even when they see that the prospect wants to buy. They ignore obvious buying signals because they are afraid that prospects might say no. They prefer preserving the pleasant conversational atmosphere to risking rejection and failure. Guerrillas at the *Principle* phase are beyond these feelings.

The best product in the world is worthless if it sits in your warehouse. If you have performed the earlier steps well, you know that your prospects need your product and can afford it. But there they are, perched on the fence. Give them that little nudge they may need to overcome their fear of acting. You will be doing them a favor.

You may feel that asking for the order may be inconsistent with fair-care-share. Don't worry. Proactive prospects will close for you, and the reactive ones are really secretly wanting you to take the initiative. Guerrillas have learned to relax, to avoid pushing, to really listen, and to relate to prospects on the prospects' terms. If you're really paying attention, guerrilla style, you'll sense when the prospect is ready, and you'll be there with the appropriate amount of decision assistance and emotional support.

Keep in mind that closing repeatedly will increase your sales, help prospects, and increase their respect for you. So don't leave until you have used at least three guerrilla closes.

Most people do not want to be pressured. They want to make their own decisions, and they resent being pushed too hard. The idea is to make them feel that buying today is the most natural, intelligent decision that they could make. Guerrillas commit these closes to memory.

Eight types of closes:

There are eight basic closes and an infinite number of variations. They all have the same objective: to give the prospect an opportunity to say, "Yes, write up the order."[1]

1. The Prescription Close

The first is called the Prescription Close. This close works well with Authority-phase prospects. You carefully probe, ask questions, summarize the problem, then prescribe the solution. "Well, based on what you've told me, I would recommend . . . Here's what you're going to need." If you have established your expertise with this prospect, you can do that. He's laid out all his specific criteria and said, "This is the problem I want to solve."

"Okay, well, you're going to need one of these, one of these, four of those, and two of these." A good salesclerk in a hardware store knows how to do that. He's pouring the stuff in a paper bag and marking the price on the outside, then handing it to you as he goes. You walk out with an armload.

2. The Action Close

In this close you *do* something that carries the decision with it. This works well with Pleasers. Pull out your pen and start filling out the order form, or phone the installer to set up an appointment. Or you say, "Well, let me see if I've got that in stock. Just a second."

You walk to the stockroom, return with the box in your arms, and ask, "Okay, where are you parked?" You know the deal is done when the prospect holds the door open for you. The Action Close requires that you do something that carries the decision.

3. The Choice Close

Here's another close for Pleaser clients. In this close, you give the prospect a minor decision to make that carries the major decision

[1] The classic book on closing is Zig Ziglar's *Secrets of Closing the Sale.*

along with it. This can be useful when breaking down a large decision into smaller, incremental decisions. You've been looking at a $15,000 automobile and the guerrilla says, "Would you like to put the stereo in the dash, or would you rather conceal it under the seat?" Now you've got this little decision to make. So you say, "Well, it would be more convenient in the dash." Not only have you bought the stereo, but of course, the car as well.

4. The Add-On Close

This close is designed for Ego prospects. The key phrase of the Add-On Close is "Now you'll also need . . ." and you propose some inexpensive option or accessory. "You'll also need one of these to keep your blade nice and sharp. They're only ten dollars." When they agree to the blade sharpener, they've bought the lawn mower.

5. The Question Close

In the Question Close, you ask a question, which, when answered, gives you permission to proceed. Depending on the questions you ask, this close will work well with Ego-, Pleaser-, and Authority-phase prospects.

To the helpful Pleaser you might ask, with your pen in hand, "What's today's date?" even though you may have written it a dozen times today. When prospects answer that question they have, in effect, given you *permission* to proceed with filling out the order form.

With an Ego you might ask, "Excuse me, how do you spell your last name?" or "What is the full name of your firm?" With an Authority you could confirm the technical specifications or another detail. When they provide the missing information, they're saying, indirectly, "Yes, I'm ready. Let's go ahead with this." You've avoided putting them on the spot by asking, "Well, do you want me to write this up or not?"

6. The Bigger Order Close

As it turns out, it is usually easier for prospects to respond to your specific request than it is for them to make the buying decision by themselves. Suggest a specific order and make it big. Researchers have found that simply asking for larger orders increases the average size of each sale, particularly with Ego- and Pleaser-phase prospects. If you ask prospects to buy ten units, they probably will not buy any more than that. If you ask them to buy one hundred units, they may buy ten, fifty, or even one hundred.

Out west, a new guy outsold every other veteran route salesperson by leaps and bounds. His manager was simply flabbergasted. "Why," he said, "you sold over a thousand *cases* and the next best salesperson sold fewer than five thousand *cans!*"

"Gee whiz!" he said. "I didn't know I could sell them by the can!"

7. The Assumptive Close

An assumption makes the buying decision seem smaller and less painful. The bigger a decision seems, the more anxious and indecisive prospects become. When you communicate your assumption that the prospect is going to go ahead, prospects feel they are not making a new decision; they are just going along with a decision that has already been made.

The Assumptive Close also makes another force work for you. Most people adjust to others' expectations. If you communicate that you do not expect them to buy, they often will not. This principle becomes clearer when you put the nonverbal message into words. Would you buy from someone who asked, "You don't want to buy anything today, do you?"

When your entire manner communicates that you expect a sale, you will often get it. Your confidence increases prospects' confidence. The buying decision seems like a natural step in the direction you are both going for.

"Excuse me a moment while I write up your order. You'll be comfortable if you wait in this chair."

8. The Today Close

Many salespeople think they are closing when they're just repeating their presentations. They talk about the benefits of their products, but do not push for immediate action. Your product's benefits will probably be the same tomorrow or next week as they are today, so why should prospects take more time to think about it?

To overcome the prospect's natural reluctance to making commitments, sell the benefits of action *now*. Some companies give discounts or premiums to people who act quickly. If your company does that, make sure you *do not mention it until this stage*. Save it to give that extra push toward getting the order. If you don't need it here, don't use it. Save it for Stage Seven, the Reward Stage.

Point out that the sooner they own this product, the sooner they'll start getting the benefits. Make these benefits as personal and specific as possible. For example, all insurance people know true stories of people who delayed buying insurance, then died or had an accident. With people who dislike shopping, stress the value of getting the shopping over with.

"It's a nice PC, but I'm just not sure. I'd better think it over."

"How many PCs have you looked at?"

"Quite a few."

"Doesn't it get tedious going from store to store?"

"It sure does."

"I'll bet this shopping has interfered with your business and your free time."

"You're darn right! I'm getting sick of it."

"Well, I've got a great cure for that problem! Take this machine home with you today. If you see one you like better in the next thirty days, just bring this one back."

"Okay."

Silence is golden

If you keep talking, no prospect can say, "I'll take it." Many salespeople talk so much that prospects cannot buy without interrupting them. As soon as you mention the order, *pause for at least ten seconds*. Silence may make you uncomfortable, but it's the best way to get prospects to respond, usually within seconds.

If you do not appear to be challenging them or using silence as a pressure tactic, prospects will respond more positively and rapidly. Smile, sit back, and let your entire manner communicate that you are courteously giving them a chance to think without feeling pressured.

If one close doesn't work, try another. Varying your close increases your chances of appealing to prospects' real motives and overcoming their resistance to buying. It also prevents win-lose confrontations. If you use the same close again and again, prospects may feel you are pushing too hard. When you master several, you can select the best closes for each situation and close repeatedly without appearing pushy. The exception is the prospect who raises an *objection* in response to a close. This tells you that it's time to backpedal, ask more questions, probe for additional criteria, and start the NaB & CaPTuRe process all over again. Continue cycling through the steps until you have an affirmative.

People are less suspicious than many salespeople believe, but they are also more sophisticated. *The public is as smart as your mother*, and you know she's no dummy. People know when you're asking them to take some action, and if they're not ready, they'll let you know. Top salespeople confirm that simple, direct, unsophisticated closes can be very effective.

Prospects in the Transaction Stage

You can't use all the guerrilla closes with all of your prospects. Certain closes are more effective with certain types.

Ego prospects

Ego prospects respond to directness and tenacity. You must prove that you are tough, so ask for the order again and again. Many Ego people will not buy until you prove your toughness by closing several times.

Vary your closes so it seems less a contest of wills. Your first close should probably be a Direct Close. Ask the Ego pointblank, "Do you want to go ahead with this?" Closes involving the Ego's image often work, because Ego people like to think of themselves as strong and decisive.

Pleaser prospects

With Pleaser prospects, do not use the Direct Close; it may make the buying decision seem too large and frightening.

Pleasers need reassurance, psychological support, and a gentle nudge. They often lack confidence in themselves and are afraid to make decisions. Provide reassurance that you sincerely do care about them, and make the buying decision seem smaller and less frightening. The we're-in-this-together type close provides reassurance and psychological support. Say something like, "I just want you to know that we're not happy unless the customer is happy. Our future depends on satisfied customers like you." The Choice and Action closes make the buying decision seem less intimidating.

Authority prospects

Authority prospects are probably the hardest to close. They prefer analysis to action and can usually find logical reasons for procrastinating. They want to study your material, invite bids from other vendors, or confer with experts. Since they respond only to facts and logic, you must make a convincing case for acting now. Traditional Balance Sheet closes are particularly useful. You lay out the facts in writing. If necessary, make two balance sheets: one comparing your product to an alternative solution to their problem, the other comparing the benefits of acting *now* versus procrastinating.

The Prescription Close can be useful if you carefully lay out a course of action that will, step by step, lead to a solution of the problems uncovered in the Need Stage. Don't bluff with the Authority. You can easily lose the sale, and more importantly, your credibility. Other closes should generally be avoided. Authority people view them as manipulative and dishonest.

The last word on closing

Guerrillas know that they've done everything right when *the customer closes the sale* for them. They must be very attentive so that they don't overshoot the point at which the prospect has made a decision, because *how* you close is not nearly as important as *when* you close.

We've seen ads in the newspaper: *"Closers Wanted!* You don't have to know how to *sell*, you just have to know how to *close."* We even get calls from nonguerrilla sales managers, asking something like, "I was wondering if you could come in here and give our guys some help on *closing.* They're really pretty sharp guys, they know the product, and they know how to present it pretty well, but they have trouble *closing*, you know. Can you come in and give them some techniques that will make them better *closers?"*

There's really nothing magical about closing. It's simply a matter of giving your prospects the *opportunity* to make a commitment at a *time* when they feel motivated to act. One of the most common errors is overshooting the close, missing that magic moment when they're ready to say yes.

The guerrilla breaks the decision down into small enough pieces, making it easy for the prospect to decide. Perhaps the most astonishing characteristic about guerrillas is that they don't consider themselves to be expert closers, but instead cause their prospects to become expert at closing.

If you're having trouble closing, it's because you're not paying attention to the signals being given to you. Guerrilla closing has more to do with recognizing when prospects are ready than it does with wringing a commitment out of them. *Closing is always best done by the customer.* Underline that thought in your mind. Make it a double underline. If you try to close before a prospect is ready, your rapport will evaporate. If you allow the prospect to close, your rapport will continue to its logical and desirable conclusion.

10
The Reward Stage

Oh, by the way

"Congratulations, you've just invested in years of the best digital sound available. You're gonna love it."

As the customer turns to leave, the guerrilla adds, "Oh, by the way, you're going to need a pair of headphones, especially when your teenagers get their hands on this new stereo. Here, take this pair with my compliments."

"Wow! Thank you for all your time and help, but the headphones, this is *wonderful!*" The customer is excited about the new stereo system, and *grateful* to the guerrilla for selling it.

This last step in the NaB & CaPTuRe selling track is the most critical, and *the one most overlooked by the competition.* Rewarding customers involves keeping something extra in reserve, congratulating your new clients, then delighting them by "throwing it in" at the last minute.

Once guerrillas have given the customer the reward, they disappear into the brush like the Lone Ranger. Hurry to your next call, help another shopper, or go hide in the stockroom. You want to be remembered for the reward, so give the customer something special to remember you by. Be warned: your customers will be so pleased they'll want to continue the conversation. Be polite, but take off.

The objective of the Reward Stage is to leave the new customer *feeling special.* One of our clients runs a very successful office supply store and is devoted to promoting environmentally responsible products. After writing up the order for a new copier, the clerk thumps his forehead and says, "Oh, I almost forgot! You're going to need some paper. Let me throw in a case, no charge. I'd like you to try this recycled copier paper; it's a bit more expensive than virgin stock, but it has a smoother finish, and besides, I don't want to mess up my paperwork."

The last thing customers remember is the guerrilla's generosity. No matter how hairy the negotiations may have been, no matter how remorseful they might feel about spending the money, even if they think they could have wangled a better deal elsewhere, the last thing the customers are left with is a feeling of surprise and conquest.

Mike Lavin runs the Berkeley Design Shop and two other sleep and kids' furniture stores in the San Francisco Bay area. When a customer purchases a complete bed set — mattress and platform frame — and the purchase has been completed, the salesperson who wrote up the sale says, "Oh, by the way, why don't you go over to our linen display and pick out a set of sheets. It's on us." He *could* have bundled a sheet set in with the package deal, but that would defeat the objective. For the reward to be effective, it must be something *beyond the customer's expectations*.

Part of this is pure reward for the customer, an expression of appreciation for the business. But, frankly, Mike knows that the average American keeps a bed for nine years, and if he treats them right, they'll come back to buy *all* their future linen at Berkeley Design Shop.

Jackpot!

Guerrillas know that everyone loves to win, so they send every customer away feeling as though they just hit the jackpot. With guerrillas, it's always everyone's lucky day. Everyone likes getting something for nothing, especially when they don't expect it. It feels like winning the lottery or getting a call from Publishers Clearing House. In the Reward Stage, guerrillas secure their position with customers by always rewarding them for their business.

Michael LeBoeuf, in his best seller *The Greatest Management Principle in the World*,[1] says that any behavior that gets rewarded gets repeated. Guerrillas build a "fifth column" of customers, a loyal underground of followers who fight for the cause.

Attention!

One of the most powerful ways to reward people who do business with you is to pay attention to them. Even something as simple as a handwritten thank-you note can be a reward. It's an old-fashioned custom that's seldom used in business, but it differentiates a guerrilla from a competitor by showing that you care.

---

[1] Michael LeBoeuf, *The Greatest Management Principle in the World* (New York: Berkley Books, 1985).

The travel industry has put the reward tactic to work as competition for the business traveler heats up. Amenities like shampoo, hair driers and minibars used to be found in only the four- and five-star hotels. Now even low-end properties pamper guests with a complimentary basket of goodies. Frequent patronage is rewarded with free upgrades, newspapers, cocktails, limo service, breakfast, or credits toward catalog merchandise.

Airlines have established special clubs and lounges where they lavish their customers with VIP check-in, comfy chairs, big-screen TVs, workstation-size phone booths, desks, conference rooms, fax machines, coffee, snacks, and a private bar. Customers *pay* a substantial annual *fee* for the *privilege* of being pampered, and will endure long connection delays in order to fly their airline of choice, even when another carrier's schedule would be more convenient, all because they're members of the club. Rewards win customers and keep them coming back.

From a weekend at a resort to a free order of fries, guerrillas have learned the power of giving something extra when they make the sale. But make sure that the customer *knows* it's a *bonus*. A guerrilla copy shop offers a courtesy telephone, marked by a large sign that says FOR OUR CUSTOMERS' CONVENIENCE, and a mail drop with a sign that reads WE'D LIKE TO SAVE YOU THE TRIP. A lumberyard gives every customer an oversized flat carpenter's pencil, imprinted with the store's name and number, but before putting it in the bag, the clerk always mentions, "These are usually a dollar, but today it's our way of saying thanks."

The right attitude

Approaching the Reward Stage with the right attitude is essential. Contrast the attitudes of two major airlines, as reflected in the way they administer their frequent-flyer programs. Both companies compete for lucrative business travelers in every major market in North America. Both programs reward customers with a free round-trip ticket after they've flown 20,000 miles.

The first airline restricts how the free ticket can be used: you must fly Monday through Thursday, stay over a weekend, and book the trip at least seven days in advance. Holidays are blacked out as well, and once the ticket is cut, it's nonnegotiable. They feel that they're giving you a free ride so you really can't complain. Their attitude is "You're a freeloader. We don't care, because *we don't have to.*"

The second airline allows its customers to use the free ticket *any* day of the week, without restriction (except for some holidays), on a space-available basis. You can book your trip as close as one hour before departure, and if your travel plans change, the ticket is *completely* negotiable for up to a year. Their attitude is "We want to do everything we can for you. You're one of *our most valued customers.*"

Both airlines are giving away an *identical* seat, but the perceived values of the rewards in the *customers'* minds are quite different. An *attitude of gratitude* is what makes the second airline so special. Perhaps that's why the first airline is losing millions, while the second just placed orders for 40 billion dollars' worth of new aircraft.

Don't get mad, get even

Jeff Slutsky of Gahanna, Ohio, author of *Streetfighting,*[2] tells a story about a local pizza chain: "There's this family chain of pizza stores in Denver; six stores, specializing in home delivery, all doing wonderfully. Nice business, until Domino's Pizza moves in. Now Domino's, as you probably know, is the undisputed number-one in pizza delivery, and they go in there with a big budget, they do a good job, and these local guys are hurtin'.

"You want to get a pizza, you look in the Yellow Pages, and the first halfway decent ad you see, you call 'em up, and you get it delivered. Well, Domino's comes in and buys a full-page ad in the phone book, with color, blue and red, and it's killin' 'em.

"As soon as the Yellow Page book comes out, these guys run a campaign that says, 'Bring us the Domino's Yellow Page ad and we'll give you two-for-one pizzas!' People were rippin' 'em out and bringin' 'em in, goin' into phone booths and rippin' 'em out. You couldn't find a Domino's ad anywhere in town!"

That's the guerrilla spirit. Guerrilla selling is an *attitude,* a philosophy, though guerrillas don't encourage vandalism, or anything unethical. It's a thought process that involves *outthinking* the competition instead of *outspending* them and recognizing that there's a world of new ideas that can help you sell.

Guerrilla selling is also a methodology. The object is more than

[2] Jeff Slutsky, *Streetfighting: Low Cost Advertising/Promotions for Your Business* (Englewood Cliffs, N.J.: Prentice-Hall, 1984). To order Jeff's book, call him at 614-337-7474.

survival. Guerrillas want to prevail, to win, to serve customers as they've never been served before. They give every customer their best shot. Sometimes they even put the Reward Stage up-front.

Free shine

Wilson was walking from his hotel to the convention center in Cincinnati on his way to give a seminar, and a kid on the sidewalk was counting, "Ninety-seven, ninety-eight, ninety-nine," then pointed to him and said, "One hundred! Congratulations, mister! Today's my birthday, and the one-hundredth person who walks past my stand gets a free shine!"

How can he say no? He expected the kid to hit his shoes a few times with a buff brush and then hit him up for a tip. But no. This kid turned out to be a real artist. He's brushing away the dirt and popping his rag and he says, "All dressed up like that you mus' be goin' somewheres *important*."

"Well, yes," Wilson says. "I'm giving a lecture today over here at the convention center."

"Well, sir! An important man like you gotta look his *best*. Better use the *beeeezwax* so this shine last a *long* time."

The kid rubs and buffs and polishes for ten minutes; the shoes look better than new. "Thank you very much, sir," the kid says with a big grin. "It's a pleasure serving you!"

Wilson stands, admires the young man's work, reaches into his pocket, and pulls out the first bill he touches. It was the first time he had ever paid twenty dollars for a shoeshine. What the heck, he thought, it was the kid's birthday, and as he walked away, he heard the kid looking up the street and counting again, "Ninety-five, ninety-six, ninety-seven . . ."

Guerrilla photography

A guerrilla bundled in Day-Glo green skiwear stood at the top of the mountain, dancing around excitedly with a camera around his neck and an order pad in hand. "Free photos today!" he shouts to the skiers as they come down off the lift. *No catch.* He would send you one *free* eight-by-ten color glossy of you and your friends looking terrific on the slopes, with Lake Tahoe in the background. If you want more copies, (and who can buy just one?) they sell for nine dollars each. We bought three!

Guerrilla service

The Nordstrom chain of department stores is famous for outstanding customer service. Near the main door of their store in Seattle, a tastefully dressed young woman stands behind a massive oak service desk. Above her on the wall, four-inch brass letters spell out ASK ME, I KNOW.

Unable to resist this challenge, we approached the information desk. "Excuse me. I was wondering if you could help us with some information?"

"Certainly!"

"How long do you bake an eleven-pound turkey?"

Without batting an eyelash, she answers, "Three hours and forty minutes, or twenty minutes a pound." We were astounded.

This guerrilla knows her stuff! At the desk is a stack of directories and phone books about two feet high. It's actually her *job* to answer *any* question that any customer might ask about anything in the store, the Westlake Plaza, the Pike Street Market, downtown Seattle, or Washington state in general. She also gives away complimentary parking tokens (normally a dollar).

You don't have to be small to be a guerrilla. The Nordstrom legend is testimony to the power of attending to tiny details.

True value

One of our clients tells about a guerrilla hardware store in Boulder, Colorado, that has a reputation for being expensive. You can find it *cheaper* just about anywhere, but if you just can't find it *anywhere* else, go to Mcguckin's Hardware.

Our client was restoring an antique drum set and had broken a lug-screw. The head was an odd square shape to fit a drum-wrench, with English threads. Companies stopped making these things fifty years ago; everything today is metric. Rummaging through parts bins in the dusty back rooms of a dozen music stores proved a major exercise in frustration.

As a last resort, he went to Mcguckin's. The shock of walking in the place was overwhelming! It was huge, brightly lit, and spotless. Everything was neatly labeled, priced, and exquisitely merchandised.

He had barely walked in when a young man in a freshly pressed green apron greeted him with raised eyebrows and asked, "Are you looking for something in particular?"

"Well, yes," he said. "I've just about given up hope, but maybe

you've got something in the way of a bolt or something that will work."
He showed the clerk the broken lug and resigned himself to enduring
the usual runaround. He was growing accustomed to being shuffled
from one clerk to another for an hour or so before being dumped out
on the street.

"Let's take a look," says the clerk, turning down a long, narrow aisle,
walled in by high steel shelf units, each containing hundreds of small
drawers. The *first* drawer he opened revealed an assortment of four-
sided-head, with a three-eighths-inch diameter chrome-plated shaft,
with English threads, lug screws!

"Now what length did you need?" he asked.

Three register clerks stood by, waiting to ring up this sizable order.
Our friend paid forty cents, which when you think about it, is an *out-
rageous* price to pay for one lousy screw. But he would have gladly paid
twenty dollars or more to repair this drum. He had already invested
weeks looking for the broken part; the Mcguckin's clerk found it in two
minutes. That's why our friend goes back, and as a home owner, he
spends a lot of money in Mr. Mcguckin's higher-priced-than-anyone-
else-in-town hardware store.

The reason is simple: lots of rewards. You can't walk down an aisle
without bumping into one of those green-aproned guerrillas. Two
thirds of Mcguckin's employees are dedicated to full-time floorwalking,
and *every* employee stocks shelves until everyone knows where every
one of over 10,000 items can be found. They are prohibited by company policy from ever using the phrase, "No, we don't have that."
Instead they say, "We'll be happy to order it for you," while serving
over 3,000 customers a day, seven days a week.

The success story of this hometown hardware can be boiled down to
three common sense things that guerrillas understand.

First, they *anticipate* the customers' needs by having a wide selection of merchandise and options available. In addition, the guerrilla is
always prepared to suggest some solution or alternative, even if it
means brokering an item or personally introducing the customer to a
competitor.

Second, they give customers *only one person to deal with.* These
guerrillas know the territory. If you want to win the respect and loyalty
of your customer, take *personal responsibility* for solving the problem
without handing it off to someone else. If this means you have to do
research, check with another department, or ask a supervisor, fine.
Guerrillas will set up a three-way conference call and keep the customer at their side and on the line as they investigate.

Third, they *add value* to commodity hardware items through display, merchandising, and service. Guerrillas know that people make buying decisions on the basis of value, not price. And everyone at every level can find ways to add value, regardless of the product. Whether it's tracing the status of an order, investigating an invoicing error, or pricing out a custom job, guerrillas remember that customer service is everyone's responsibility.

The bad news is that American business is increasingly being dominated by coupon printers, discounters, and offshore manufacturers. In this economic environment, *service is the only arena where the guerrilla can compete effectively*.

The good news is that *people will gladly pay, and pay handsomely, for exceptional treatment*. That means rendering service that never sends them away frustrated, service that surpasses the norm, service that surprises and delights, service that solves their problems. Such service will be the key to profitability for the handful of guerrillas who get it right.

11
Guerrilla Tracking

Closing future sales

By rewarding your customers and staying with them, you are closing your future sales before you make them. Guerrillas are always thinking in terms of future sales because that's where the real profits are, and once they've created a new customer, they never let him out of their sights. This is called tracking.

Guerrillas use *tracking* to achieve consistent success. The commissions from the first sale are glorious, to be sure, but they're a pittance compared with the potential earnings from repeat and referral business, year after year. A satisfied customer is the best source of referral sales, and guerrillas know that they have to ask for referrals and reward them.

Tracking is the first step toward future selling opportunities. Though not part of the six-stage NaB & CaPTuRe track, it is an indispensable part of being a guerrilla. Tracking guarantees an endless supply of customers and commissions. This is where the guerrilla secures the future, closing future sales before you ever open them.

Tracking separates guerrillas from ordinary salespeople. Like an air traffic controller, the guerrilla tracks the order the way radar tracks the flight path of an aircraft. This includes quietly shadowing the order through to delivery, keeping accurate and careful records, trailing your customers' needs, all of which leads you to referrals and future sales from loyal customers.

Shadowing

Shadowing means following through on the order within their organization, from the signed paperwork all the way to delivery of the product. Guerrillas do this discreetly, without being seen by everyone in the organization. They never get in the way or become a nuisance to the folks in shipping or accounting, but they check up and make certain that the product is delivered *exactly* as ordered. This means exactly *when* ordered, exactly *what* was ordered, and shipped exactly *as* ordered. They insist on being notified by shipping, accounting, or field service of any delay, any change that would violate the customers' expectations. Guerrillas do *everything* they can to eliminate any difficulties that arise, and take *personal* responsibility for reporting problems to the customer. If a product is out of stock, the customer gets the bad news from the guerrilla rather than receiving a shipment and discovering that part of the order has been back-ordered or delayed. They check in with their friends in low places and refresh their recon regularly.

Delivery meeting

Whenever possible, *the guerrilla delivers the first order personally,* or visits the customer the day it arrives to ensure that everything is perfect. They check up on installation as it proceeds. This practice ensures a level of quality control that is unparalleled. Timing is critical. If a piece is defective or damaged in transit, the guerrilla files the report and expedites the replacement. The customer never gets a chance to complain.

Most salespeople are eager to move on to the next mission, the next conquest, the next prospect, and skip this critical step — but not the guerrilla. A well-executed delivery meeting secures the guerrilla's position with the client, helping assure *future sales* to this customer and gaining *referred leads* for the guerrilla as well.

The delivery meeting is in many ways a service call. It starts with the guerrilla personally presenting the product to the new client or delivering the contract that initiates the service.

First, the guerrilla reaffirms the client's reasons for buying and acknowledges the good judgment shown by the selection of his or her firm as vendor. The next step is to discuss any particulars concerning the product. The guerrilla explains the operation of the product or service to the end users, meets with others who may be responsible for maintenance or service, and ties up any loose ends. Guerrillas take care to explain and answer questions fully, and often leave written instructions and a list of names to call.

MicroLam, a company in Boise, Idaho, manufactures laminated wooden beams for the construction trade. A plastic-coated card, printed with the office and *home* phone numbers of the sales representative, the production engineer, vice presidents, and even the president, is stapled right to the beam. Anyone trying to install one can call someone, day or night, for technical support.

The final portion of the delivery call should be with the Decider or Purchaser, to thank him or her again for the business and to reaffirm the continuing service to follow. *This is also the ideal time to ask for referred leads.*

Properly handled, the delivery interview is the beginning of a solid relationship. After a smooth start, future calls and larger orders become easier the next time around. Guerrillas know that when they leave, everyone is satisfied and will stay satisfied.

Depending on the goods or services sold, the delivery interview may take the better part of a working day, and competent salespeople never try to squeeze this call in. They plan carefully and allow plenty of time, knowing that this interview can be the foundation for building future growth. *This process should be repeated anytime a regular customer orders something new or out of the ordinary.*

Record keeping

Unfortunately, filling out reports is often viewed as one of the least satisfying aspects of selling. Guerrillas know that they must understand and control their own sales activity in order to maximize their production. Guerrillas keep accurate records, including complete expense, sales activity, and call reports, on a regular basis. They carefully monitor their own performance and closely watch trends and averages. For the guerrilla, it is one of the most important aspects of the selling process. The smart ones share this information with the rest of the office, charting everyone's production on a bulletin board or dry-erase marker board, weekly or daily, so they can see how they stand among peers.

Reports are required by the sales manager to help "make operations better in the future," and if the sales manager can use these reports for this purpose, so can the guerrilla. To illustrate, we will look at several reports and demonstrate how they can put money in the bank for you.

In each report, there is information that is useful to you and your firm. Even if you are the entire firm, you'll need to keep these records.

Expense and sales activity reports

There is usually one page for each day of the week, Monday through Sunday, and one for the week's total.

Expense report

The expenses section of the weekly report form usually includes:

1. auto mileage
2. cost of meals
3. room expenses
4. miscellaneous expenses
5. number of calls made, grouped by type of call

You'll need information from (1) through (4) when you file your income taxes. Several things can be learned from this part of the weekly report.

Once you determine what your expenses should be for a typical week, you can study each week's report to determine if your spending is out of line. If expenses are more than expected, then you are either living more extravagantly than you should or your travel planning is inefficient. If expenses are lower than expected, you may be spending too much time in the office and not enough time in the field.

Also look at trends in expenses. It costs nearly twice as much to stay in New York or San Francisco as it does to stay in Seattle or Miami. Does the potential income from this account justify the investment? A trip to Cheyenne, Wyoming, may be less glamorous but more profitable. A smart practice is to divide total expenses by the orders written and track the four-week rolling average expense per order. Even if your expenses are reimbursed by the company, this will encourage you to go after the high-margin, high-profit business.

The record of the total number of calls, recorded by type of call, can also be instructive. By "type of call" we mean cold call, first interview, presentation, phone call, group meeting, close, delivery, or follow-up. Guerrillas can tell from this data whether they are spending too much time making some types of calls and not enough time making others.

Although the number of each type of call made each day or week will vary greatly, guerrillas will soon know whether the variation is normal or whether they have avoided calls with which they have difficulty.

Sales activity report

Here, salespeople report the name, location, and dollar amount of all business written for the period. It should also include projected delivery dates, if applicable, and track the weekly average sale and four-week rolling average sale. Sales activity reports tell you who's buying what, and can help the guerrilla spot hot trends.

Call reports

Almost all salespeople prepare call reports, on which they indicate the purpose and result of each sales call. Some firms use a single form for all types of calls; others use a different form for each. This report includes the date and time of each sales call, the type of call, and a brief description of the result of the call.

By reviewing the order of calls by location, guerrillas can determine if their call planning is effective. For example, if they find that the first three calls on Monday were in Miami and the last two in Boca Raton, they know that the trip was better planned than if the order of calls required trips back and forth between cities.

The report also shows at a glance whether certain types of calls are more successful than others. If this is the case, the guerrilla can reexamine the differences.

Since summaries of the activities reports of all sales personnel are often sent to each salesperson, guerrillas can learn how their activities compare with those of the most successful people in the company. For example, they can see how more experienced people divide their time between the various types of calls they complete each week.

Prospect report

If the first call does not result in a sale, the salesperson usually completes only the top portion of the form and the "Remarks" section at the bottom and indicates the date of the planned call-back. All of this information is useful for subsequent sales calls. The data at the top of the form includes pertinent information about the prospect. The information in the "Remarks" section is usually more personal; if something unusual happened during the first visit or if the prospect revealed some particular interests or hobbies, these would be noted there.

Information of this nature makes a second call more personal and demonstrates the guerrilla's personal interest. Indicating the planned call-back date forces you to plan future sales calls and travel. It also serves as a "tickler" to remind you that another call is needed on this particular prospect and when it should be made.

On occasion, the sales call may not result in selling a product or service, but the salesperson may have learned a great deal about the prospect's present and future needs. In such a case, the salesperson also completes another portion of the prospect report, recording all pertinent information about the prospect's needs. On the guerrilla's next visit, this information will be extremely useful.

The prospect report may also include an estimated dollar amount the salesperson expects the prospect to buy and an estimate of the probability of closing. These figures can be multiplied together to give the salesperson a "pending" total. For example, if a prospect is considering a $10,000 machine, and the guerrilla figures he has a 75 percent chance of closing within the next ninety days, he would be said to have $7,500 "pending" in that account. By doing a running total of all pending business each month and monitoring whether the numbers increase or decrease, the guerrilla can quickly see if he needs to concentrate on developing new prospects or closing existing ones.

Some companies put prospects into three categories: Group A is expected to close this month; Group B is expected to close this quarter; and Group C is expected to close within a year. Guerrillas manage their prospecting activity to maintain a balance between the number of A, B, and C prospects.

Proposal report

Once the guerrilla has made a formal sales proposal to a prospective client, a proposal report should be completed. The form used for the proposal report is similar to the prospect report. The proposal report is useful as a tickler to remind the guerrilla that a proposal has been made and that after a reasonable amount of time a call-back is necessary to close the sale.

The proposal report should include any pertinent remarks made by the prospect during the proposal presentation, including objections or concerns expressed about the proposal or things the prospect specifically liked about it. It could also include information about who is involved in the purchase decision and when the prospect expects the decision to be made. This information will be helpful in closing the sale.

Prospect and "tickler" files were discussed in chapter 2. We mention them again here to remind you that they are an essential part of your tracking activity.

Trailing

Guerrillas "trail" their customers to assure that the product not only was delivered as promised, but *performs as expected*. Here's how it's done: The final comment of the delivery interview should be "I'll be checking back in a week or so to make sure everything is working as planned. It's a routine part of our quality assurance. That would be the morning of the tenth; is that convenient for you?" If the product sold is new to the employees or a bit complicated, the new customer will be glad to know that the guerrilla will be checking in on a given date to answer questions. This follow-up visit should be made within a few days of the product being put into service, and certainly not more than two weeks later. Contact with *users* at this stage is particularly important. If they have any questions or difficulties, these must be dealt with now or your future business is in jeopardy.

Trailing is particularly important if the product itself has been delivered by truck or by someone other than the salesperson. If the product sold has had to be installed, the trailing call-back would properly come shortly after the installation work is complete. The most important point here is not *when* the call is made, but that it *is* made.

Consistency

Xerox built an empire from creative and persistent advertising over the years, so that the word "Xerox" became synonymous with "photocopy." Guerrillas want to get their customers conditioned in much the same way, so that customers will think of them automatically whenever they require additional service. They do this by not letting the customers forget them. Keeping in touch is possible through a variety of creative ways.

Nine proven guerrilla trailing methods include:

1. A short note after delivery, asking if everything is all right
2. Restating availability by a simple phone call
3. Impromptu goodwill calls
4. Cards at Christmas and Thanksgiving; guerrillas also send them on the more offbeat holidays like Halloween, Columbus Day, and Presidents' Day

5. Brief telephone calls on items of mutual interest, such as a customer's mention in local newspapers
6. Fliers about product changes or other information, accompanied by a handwritten note
7. Miscellaneous but related information such as company announcements or sales progress reports
8. Letters containing newspaper items of interest to the customer
9. Notices of achievement awards and honors earned by the salesperson; these are best sent by the sales manager, not the salesperson

Of course, every customer is different, and it's only natural that large-account, regular customers get more attention than smaller, occasional customers. Some types of sales, a new bookkeeping system, for example, or new word processors for an entire department, may require several postsale sessions and numerous call-backs, whereas other sales are comparatively routine. But even the most modest sale requires some keeping in touch. Quite apart from maintaining your own reputation as a courteous and dependable guerrilla, your call-backs to smaller customers could lead, through referral, to other customers in the same area. Just as easily, slighting a customer because he seems unimportant might cause you to lose a large order someday.

Guerrillas never ignore a customer account. They do what is required to nurture and expand all their business, and they look upon the time it takes for call-backs as a valued opportunity to build customer goodwill and an *investment* in their own future.

The important thing is to make a path leading to referrals and more business. This way the sales cycle can repeat itself over and over again, giving you a never ending source of new customers.

Future sales

The competition feels that in large metropolitan areas they can always find new prospects, and may think that they don't have to bother keeping in touch with old customers. But guerrillas know the value of repeat sales, and this gives them a tremendous advantage.

With competition growing daily, new customers are not as easy to find as they once were. It makes sense to build a portfolio of repeat buyers. Guerrillas prefer vertical growth to selling to a large number of

new customers, and repeat sales are *far more profitable* because of re-
duced marketing costs.

Customer loyalty

There is no mystery about customer loyalty. People simply like to
deal with people they know and trust. Customers like knowing that
someone who understands their needs or problems will be available to
help. That's why we like to go to a favorite restaurant or buy clothes at
the same shop from the same salesperson year after year.

Guerrillas who give their customers above-and-beyond service are
always welcomed back. Customers give repeat business to these salespeople because they are satisfied. They know they can count on outstanding service. They understand that these salespeople feel a sense of
loyalty to them, and they like dealing with familiar faces.

By tracking every order from "cradle to grave," you're well on your
way to a prosperous and secure future as a guerrilla.

12
The Guerrilla Selling Arsenal

High-tech, high-touch guerrilla

The modern guerrilla must learn to deploy the new technology of modern business warfare with "high touch." Like laser-guided "smart" bombs, these weapons can help you target hot prospects, maneuver into new territory, and capture market share.

Information, please

Information is the new business high ground, and it's available to anyone for the asking. In his book *Powershift*, Alvin Toffler contends that while in the past the world was divided into East and West, the new global business community will be divided into *fast* and *slow*. The ability to quickly *retrieve* and *manipulate* information is one of the keys to the guerrilla attack.

Guerrillas know that most of their competitors do not have a systematic method for keeping track of vital customer information. The average business person spends *over three hours each week looking for misplaced information*. That's over four weeks' lost selling time each year! The three-by-five cards in a file box system is only a beginning for today's guerrilla, and you will soon want to automate it. Still, the simple manual system *used consistently* will be more effective than an automated system used haphazardly. The guerrilla who makes the effort to electronically automate customer files has a tremendous selling advantage.

A guerrilla we met in Nova Scotia supplies plastic pipe and fittings to the fisheries industry. Sitting down with a customer, he links up with his main office computer by phone, using his laptop PC and a modem.

He checks the inventory for each item being ordered, and if something is out of stock, he can discuss substitutions right there with the customer. Each inventory item is flagged when sold, so there are *no more frustrating back-orders*. When the process is complete, the home office computer prints the packing slip and the warehouse crew starts loading the truck even before this guerrilla has finished saying goodbye. In a market where it's common to wait *weeks* for *everything*, this company has built its reputation on next-day delivery.

The basics

It's time to wake up and smell the coffee, but if you haven't mastered the basics of computer literacy, word processing, spreadsheets, and database management, you're not alone. Millions of professionals have yet to become computer literate. What an *opportunity!*

The portable computer has become the M-16 of guerrilla selling. A PC allows you to fire off a hundred letters to customers with a touch of a button. It can review the buying patterns of a thousand companies in a matter of minutes, allowing you to be in just the right place at just the right time, getting the order from just the right person. The same PC can help manage your time, tabulate your travel expenses, graph your presentation, and even write your reports.

PC hardware

Look for something small and light, something that you wouldn't mind carrying all day in the field. Stay away from the cheap machines; you want something rugged. You can easily find a PC for under $2,000 that will do everything you need. The screen should display a full twenty-four lines. You really don't need color in a portable PC, monochrome is fine, but it should have at least VGA standard graphics for spotting trends and to ease eyestrain.

Shop for a keyboard that feels right under your hands, not too small, although you'll get used to whatever you use regularly. If you already have a desktop model, look for a portable with a similar feel. You'll need to work with many customer files, so a hard disk is a must. The bigger the better, 20 to 50 megabytes at least, and ask for at least one megabyte of RAM. The CPU should be a '286 or the faster '386sx, and as of this writing, even the Intel '486 is being built into some high-end laptops. Ask about battery life. At this writing, three hours is considered good, but you can also use "battery saver" utility programs that reduce the power drain from the hard disk. Ask about a car lighter adaptor as well. An internal modem will allow you to connect the computer to others from a hotel room, a pay phone, or even from your car's cellular phone.

Software

Word processor software turns your computer into a powerful type-writer for creating, editing, printing, and storing correspondence, proposals, and other written material. Use the word processing program your office uses. They're all good, although some are slightly better than others for different applications. The most important consideration is the ability to transfer files between the field and your home office system, either by swapping disks or connecting over the phone with a modem. An excellent integrated system that combines several applications, from word processing to tracking clients, is MS Works[1] for either a Macintosh or a DOS PC.

Your Rolodex is a simple form of manual database, and a database management program allows you to store, retrieve, and organize all those scraps of information electronically. You can create a letter with a word processor, then send it to everyone in the database that fits any set of criteria you want to select.

You could create a custom tracking system from scratch, using products like dBase III+ or FoxBase, but it probably won't be worth the time. You really need a database management package designed *specifically* for sales.

Your goal is to transfer the information from your customer files into the computer. At a minimum, you need a place for the company name, key contact names, billing address, shipping address, last contact date, next contact date, and a notes area for keeping track of what they ordered, how much, when, at what price, and other relevant details. Even simple off-the-shelf software like Konetix's Client Manager[2] can get you started for under a hundred dollars. Type in any key information, and every one of your customers fitting that description pops on-screen. The software also allows the guerrilla to merge customers' names and addresses with letters created with most word processing programs, including WordPerfect, MS Word, and WordStar, and automatically prints envelopes or mailing labels.

[1] Call Microsoft at 1-800-426-9400 for more information.
[2] Call Konetix at 1-800-326-2276 for more information.

The more sophisticated database management programs are well worth the investment. We suggest you look at The Prospecting Planner[3] by Excel, PCAT[4] by Arlington Software Systems, and Sales Ally[5] by Scherrer Resources to get a feel for what they can do.

Some of the more powerful and expensive software packages like ACT![6] from Contact Software International combine several functions in one integrated system. This software has a full-function word processor *built in*, with an 80,000-word spell-checker. The database displays 73 fields on two well-designed screens for tracking even the most sophisticated customers, and pull-down menus make everything one-keystroke simple. The software will produce call reports, expense reports, activity reports, and custom reports, and an array of clock and calendar functions can make the guerrilla's life a lot easier. There's an alarm function to remind you of important appointments, which works even if you're using a different program. Task-list reports remind the guerrilla of important calls, meetings, and things to do. The system has day-at-a-glance and week-at-a-glance schedules and will print a daily list of prospects to be called, including names and phone numbers, and connected to a modem, *it will even dial the call for you*.

Guerrilla direct

For electronic guerrilla prospecting, there are several on-line computer databases available. This means with your PC, a modem, and your telephone you can tap into the world. These information databases are a quick, affordable way to target opportunities for business-to-business sales locally, nationally, and even internationally. Dun's Sales Prospecting[7] lets you conveniently order printed lists of companies for your direct mail, telemarketing, and other sales activities. You can target companies by specifying industry, company size, and geographic location. Data are extracted from the Dun & Bradstreet *Dun's Market Identifiers* and *Dun's International Market Identifiers* databases, con-

[3] You can contact Excel at 213-430-9488.
[4] Call Arlington Software Systems at 203-230-1773.
[5] Call Scherrer Resources at 215-242-8751.
[6] ACT! is a registered trademark of Contact Software International. Call 1-800-365-0606 for more information.
[7] For additional information call Dun & Bradstreet at 1-800-422-4664.

taining *information on over eight million businesses* worldwide. The Sales Prospecting service will generate a list that matches your criteria, displaying the essential information in one of four output formats: mailing list, targeted mailing list, telemarketing list (United States only), or company profile. Generating a list of companies costs only nine dollars for the search, plus a charge for each company listing ranging between eighteen cents and two dollars per item.

Hot off the presses

You can also use newswires like Infomaster[8] or the Dow Jones News and Information Service[9] to track a target company. By setting up an electronic clipping file in the computer, you will automatically receive the text of any published articles that mention the targeted firm by name, such as press releases, patents issued to the company, or general news stories about that firm, even the company's daily stock prices. The same service can be used to shadow the *competition*.

Newswire services like Nexis can help the guerrilla track the impact of outside events that might affect business. For example, if the government is considering the approval of a new drug, it could represent a considerable threat or a terrific opportunity. The computer can automatically clip articles about a specified topic to appear in your electronic mailbox daily.

On-line services are also useful for making your own airline and travel arrangements. Hotel and car-rental reservations can be confirmed or altered the same way. You can even check the weather at your destination. You can send electronic mail instantly to other users of the network, perhaps the home office, a vendor, or another sales rep. The system will hold the message until the recipient calls in. EasyLink[10] offers access to these and many other research services by modem, starting at twenty-five dollars a month.

The guerrilla 500

Fortune magazine and the MZ Group publish the *Fortune* 500 Prospector,[11] a combination software package and database on a disk, which, according to a company brochure, ". . . gives you the infor-

---

[8] For additional information call 1-800-422-4664.
[9] Available through EasyLink at 1-800-321-MSGS.
[10] Call EasyLink Customer Service at 1-800-435-7375.
[11] Contact the MZ Group at 1-800-927-1300.

mation you need to track down your hottest prospects in the *Fortune* 500 in an easy-to-use database software package." It provides the names, titles, addresses, and phone numbers of as many as fifteen key executives, over 13,500 in all. Complete financial information, business descriptions, and industry statistics are included, along with a built-in word processor. You can add contacts from your own files and use the software to send personalized form letters and to print envelopes, mailing labels, and even Rolodex cards. *InfoWorld* magazine called it ". . . a godsend to corporations that target big-gun corporations and need a practical way to manipulate the data."

Reach out and touch someone

The telephone continues to be a powerful selling tool, and with the average cost of an industrial sales call approaching $200, the modern guerrilla uses the telephone extensively, and *properly*. For some really hot phone tips read George Walther's best-selling book *Phone Power*.[12]

Guerrilla headgear

A must for desk-bound guerrillas is the headset phone. Yeah, we know. They're a pain in the neck. Heavy, clunky, chaining the user to the desk with that damn cord! Well, not anymore. Hello Direct[13] will make you an instant convert with its line of high-fidelity headsets that weigh less than a fountain pen. They even offer a *wireless* headset phone for *under* $250. The guerrilla can keep a customer on-line while checking inventory, researching an invoice, or taking an order. The Sharper Image[14] sells a wireless unit that has an *FM stereo radio built in*, so you can rock out when you're not on the phone. A great stress reducer in noisy offices.

At the tone . . .

Guerrillas have also learned the power of making it easy for potential customers to call *them*. If you can't always be in the office to take

---

[12] Available from George R. Walther, Inc., 1-800-843-8353.
[13] Ask for Hello Direct's free catalog of high-tech phone gadgets and equipment at 1-800-444-3556.
[14] Contact the Sharper Image at 1-800-344-4444 for a free catalog.

customers' calls, consider using an answering machine or voice-mail system, but make *sure the system is responsive to customers' needs*. One of the worst examples we've heard recently said, "Thank you for calling XYZ Company. We are sorry, but our office is now closed. Please call between the hours of eight-thirty and five-thirty, Central Standard Time." Why bother? They just frustrated a potential customer.

Encourage your customers to call *anytime* and leave a message, place an order, or ask a question, then get back to them as soon as possible. In your outbound message, include the company name, your name, an explanation of when you will be back at your desk, and instructions for the caller. You might say, "I'm sorry, I'm out of the office all morning, but if you leave your name and number at the tone, I'll get back to you this afternoon." *Change* your outbound message *regularly;* three times a day is about right. Update it *every* time you retrieve messages. People often resent talking to a machine because they've heard the same recording a dozen times. Let them know what's going on from day to day and *when* they should expect to hear from you.

If you really are unavailable, *always* give them an alternative course of action: "Dial O and an operator will redirect your call", or "My assistant can be reached at extension (number)" or "You can page me on my beeper at (pager number)." Let them know what's going on, when you'll return, and what other options they have. A guerrilla in Montana left this recording on his machine: "Thanks for calling. I'll be fishin' for two weeks until the twenty-eighth. If your need is urgent, you can call (another distributor) at (their number). You'll get a real live person who will be happy to help you immediately. There will be no messages taken." Voice-mail systems like Audex[15] or GTE Tele-messenger offer a number of advantages over answering machines. Using a push-button phone, customers can dial particular digits to hear preprogrammed options like "Dial 1 to hear more information, dial 2 to place an order, dial 3 to talk to a representative, or dial 4 to speak to a service technician." These systems allow you to expedite the customer's call without having a platoon of telephone operators on duty. Customers prefer the control of being able to select their own options to being left in no-man's-land on hold. A guerrilla doesn't need a battery of expensive hardware to use voice mail, and when you consider that 70 *percent of business calls fail to reach their intended party on the*

[15]Call AT&T at 1-800-222-0400 for details about *Audex* voice mail.

first attempt, it can be a tremendous advantage. Check with your local phone company about the availability of central office services.

One way or another, *be there* for your customers when they call. We recently called a company that claims in its magazine ad to be "the nation's leading provider of voice messaging service." At six o'clock on a Saturday evening, no answer. Not even a recording! This is the kind of ridiculous mistake a guerrilla would never make.

1-800-We-LoveU

Guerrillas make it even easier for customers to call by offering an 800 number. Prospects are *seven times as likely to phone if the call is toll-free.*[16] And you don't have to be a big-budget company to offer 800 service. It's surprisingly inexpensive, but it does pay to shop around. Most long-distance carriers offer measured inbound 800-number service, where you pay *only* for the calls you receive. AT&T calls its service Readyline[17], Sprint calls its service Fonline 800,[18] and either one can give your business the "800" advantage for a base charge of about twenty dollars a month, plus about twenty cents a minute or *less.* Rates may be lower in some states. The number can be programmed to ring into any existing phone line in the United States, so you don't need a special line, and as your business grows, your 800 number can move with you. Unless you can get a custom number that is a complete acronym, like 1-800-SOFTWARE or 1-800-FLOWERS, stay away from clever combinations like 1-800-777-1234. People *think* they will remember them and then forget. Better to have a number they *have* to write down, like ours: 1-800-247-9145.

Third-party fulfillment

You can even give your customers the *convenience* of an 800 number *without the expense* by using a fulfillment service. These companies will let you *advertise their 800 number as if it were your own,* coded with a special extension. "Operators are standing by" twenty-four hours a day. These firms will stock your products, answer your calls like an answering service, write up the orders, pack and ship the boxes, deposit the funds into your bank account, and forward the finished paperwork, all for a fixed percentage of sales or a flat fee per order. A local com-

---

[16] According to AT&T promotional literature.
[17] Call AT&T at 1-800-222-0400 for details about 800 Readyline.
[18] Call Sprint at 1-800-877-4020 about Fonline 800.

pany will usually give you the best service at the best price, so pick a company nearby.

While you are out

Guerrillas know that they don't make any money sitting around the office waiting for the phone to ring. A paging service allows customers to find you even when you're out of touch. For about twenty-five dollars a month in most metropolitan markets, a beeper can notify you of important calls and maintain a closer link with the office. Some are as small as a fountain pen and can be set to vibrate discreetly in your pocket when they go off. For a nominal charge of about 50 percent of the monthly base rate, most vendors will add an optional "voice mailbox" to the pager, allowing callers to leave a detailed recorded message as well as notifying you of their attempt to call. Some services offer even more sophisticated features, such as a digital read-out that displays the caller's number or a typed message up to twenty characters in length.

Guerrillas who travel extensively might consider a nationwide satellite paging service like SkyPager.[19] For about seventy dollars a month, you can be paged almost anywhere in the United States, in over two hundred major markets, and the voice mailbox can be added for another twenty dollars. So while you're attending to a customer in Cleveland, a prospect in Portland can page you directly, even if the home office is in Houston.

We've seen one guerrilla ask his secretary to page him at a specific time, when he would be right in the middle of his presentation to a new prospect. He excused himself to return the call, assuring the prospect that the firm would be receiving the same level of prompt, personal service in the future.

Pocket phone booth

Cellular technology has gotten smaller than Maxwell Smart's shoe. Some fold-up models we've seen would easily fit in your shirt pocket. The serious guerrilla keeps one handy for a quick-draw response to customer calls. Depending on the market and the time of day, cellular time costs anywhere from forty cents to as little as three cents a minute. Here again, it pays to shop around; prices are dropping daily, and two stores in the same mall are selling the same equipment with a hundred

---

[19]Call SkyTel at 1-800-456-3333 for more information about SkyPager service.

dollars difference in price. Stay tuned for changes in this technology.*
Motorola's new Iridium phone system, scheduled to come into service
in 1995, will employ a system of satellites that will allow these pocket
phones to be used *anywhere on the planet.*

Just the fax

Facsimile is another example of a technology that has overtaken the
American business battlefield, and these devices are even *more* perva-
sive with overseas customers. Just in case you've been on *another
planet* for the last few years, a fax machine allows you to send a photocopy of a document over the phone in a matter of seconds. No ex-
cuses. Guerrillas can equip their office with a no-frills fax machine for
under three hundred dollars. It's enough to give Federal Express a case
of heartburn.

A rep for Sprint became that company's leading guerrilla by offering
to fax his prospects a one-page written rate comparison, putting them
up against other long-distance companies. Within minutes he calls
back, asking the prospect, then and there, if it makes sense for them to
keep paying too much for their long-distance service. He takes the order over the phone, then faxes a confirmation back to the new customer, all within the span of a few minutes.

Guerrillas on the road insist that the home office fax their phone
messages rather than calling the hotel. By the time a customer inquiry
has been handled by a chain of telephone receptionists, it's often man-
gled beyond recognition. A neatly typed list faxed to the hotel is much
easier to work from and less likely to include omissions or errors. If the
message comes in after business hours, guerrillas *respond* by fax as
well, answering the customer's question overnight while the competition is asleep.

Fax is particularly helpful in international business, where the pos-
sibility for misunderstanding across language barriers and cultures is an
important factor. Guerrillas confirm all international voice communications with fax. In some countries, particularly Australia, New Zea-
land, and Canada, a company *must* use fax to be taken seriously.

---

* For ongoing updates on the latest guerrilla weapons, subscribe to *The Guerrilla Selling
Newsletter.* Call 1-800-247-9145 for a complimentary copy.

When it absolutely . . .

And forget next-day delivery. Associated Air Freight has fired the first shot in the battle for overnight delivery. By calling a single toll-free number, twenty-four hours a day, seven days a week, guerrillas are now arranging for *same-day delivery*[20] of urgent documents, vital replacement parts, or essential equipment.

Getting smart

Smart guerrillas will combine these technologies in creative ways, bringing new meaning to the phrase "close to the customer." We recently received a catalog from a mail-order office supply house, inviting us to fax in our order via their 1-800-FAX-LINE.

A real estate agent in Oakland uses a car phone and portable fax to receive details from the Multiple Listing Service while touring with a prospect in the field. Several times she has beaten out other buyers by faxing in an offer, closing the deal in the time it took the other sales agent to drive back to the office.

Joe and Judy Sabah, a husband and wife team in Denver, have made a science out of getting on radio talk shows all over the country to promote their books on *How to Get the Job You Really Want*.[21] First they create a one-page billboard brochure with PageMaker software on a Macintosh computer, then program the computer's internal fax card to send it overnight to a database of radio stations. They've built a list of over 850 talk-format radio programs around the country, including their producers and their schedules. The call-in interviews are conducted by phone, from their home, and the 800 number they give out provides listeners an easy way to order their books. In three years their fulfillment service has shipped over 17,000 orders.

You think that's slick? SprintFax and EasyLink even offer an enhanced fax service. With one dial-up and *no extra hardware*, a guerrilla can fax contracts, product information, drawings, photographs, high-res graphics, or anything else to a whole list of destination numbers.[22] It's perfect for updating price lists, new product introductions, or special promotions. All can be in the hands of the field sales force (or customers) in seconds. The same service allows you to send and receive *telex* messages using your PC and modem.

---

[20]Call 1-800-SAME-DAY or write to Associated Air Freight, Inc., 3333 Hyde Park Road, New Hyde Park, NY 11042.
[21]Call them at 303-722-7200 for more information.
[22]Call 1-800-248-EFAX for details.

Talking house

Real estate agents across the country are putting houses on the air and off the market. A tape loop, combined with an AM radio transmitter about the size of a shoebox, broadcasts the properties' vital statistics. The "For Sale" sign on the lawn tells drive-bys which radio station to tune in to hear a ninety-second summary of features and the price. The service weeds out the serious buyer from the person who's just shopping around, instantly qualifying serious prospects.

Video brochure

Another high-tech option is the video brochure. Customers are more video oriented than ever before and are increasingly relying on this medium for buying decisions. The average American spends nearly seven hours a day with the television set turned on, and over three quarters of American homes have a VCR.

This is a low-cost medium — under five dollars for a ten-minute tape, plus production costs, which run about a thousand dollars a minute these days. Remember shorter is better. Videos can introduce a small company to prospective buyers, saving the expense of a direct call and making them look big-time.[23] Some automobile dealers are offering take-home video test drives, allowing customers to educate themselves on model features without the showroom pressure. A guerrilla travel agent produces dream-vacation travelogues to promote package tours. Slide presentations[24] can easily be transferred to video with a soundtrack added, and distributed directly to prospects. Guerrillas can use a portable combination TV/VCR and videotape to support their presentations, taking their prospects on a TV tour of the plant, demonstrating products too big to carry, or presenting "talking head" testimonials. Many offices now have VCRs as standard office equipment. Check ahead; it may save you the time and annoyance of carrying and setting up your own hardware.

---

[23] For a professional-looking video that won't cost you an arm and a leg, call Rob Sommer at The Producers' Corner, 619-929-1019.
[24] Contact your local Kodak dealer, or call 1-800-44KODAK, Ext. 899, for a free brochure on what slides can do for you.

In group selling, guerrillas might even use a video projector to make a big-screen impression.[25] Some of the new single-tube projectors are designed to be portable, like the MagnaByte 2002 from Telex.[26] It's small enough to take on an airplane and even features a built-in VHS tape player.

Clipboard computers

Perhaps you're one of the thousands of guerrillas who have never learned to type. If all this high-tech revolution has made you a bit cyberphobic, consider a new technology developed by a start-up company called GO, in Foster City, California. They've come up with a new way of interacting with computers, based not on the keyboard, but on the pen. In the PenPoint System, a large liquid-crystal screen and a small stylus have replaced the keyboard and mouse. You write directly on the etched-glass screen as you would on a legal pad. The system software recognizes carefully printed letters, making it ideal for guerrillas on the go. Sony and Canon have been selling similar devices in Japan for years, and virtually every major computer manufacturer is working on one of its own.

What's next? Computerized voice recognition software that can take dictation faster than most people can type.

Low-tech guerrilla with high-touch weapons

Keep in mind that you needn't load yourself down with a lot of expensive gadgets to be an effective guerrilla. It's easy to get caught up in the hardware. We've heard sales managers bemoan the day their operation was automated, because the reps click away the day at the keyboard instead of making calls. David with a sling can bring down Goliath every time, but you have to get out into the battlefield and give it a

---

[25]Contact Electrohome about its big-screen projection systems at 1-800-265-2171. In Canada, 519-744-7111.
[26]Call Telex at 612-887-5513 for information.

shot. "The only weapon my guerrillas need to carry is a pen!" one manager said emphatically. "That's all it really takes to write an order."

Guerrillas know that they must balance the high-tech with high-touch. They must be more sensitive to the subjective needs of everyone they meet. In addition to the hardware, guerrillas include several high-touch weapons in their arsenal.

1. Reconnaissance

Gather as much intelligence about your prospects as you possibly can. Even the smallest scrap of information can be valuable when it helps you relate. Most adults respond to a salesperson in predictable ways. When you first meet, pay close attention to their personalities. Watch for different phases of the Mind Map. Adjust your style to get the maximum cooperation from your prospect.

2. Creativity

Always be thinking of new ways to meet prospects. Guerrillas are contrarists. Try doing the opposite of what other sales people do: Z to A. Think up creative ways to finance your product or service. Get new ideas from sales managers, seminars, other salespeople, financial people, bankers, and CPAs.

3. Enthusiasm

A basic rule of journalism and guerrilla selling is "Don't tell the good news on page one." Hold your enthusiasm for your product until the Presentation Stage. First, thoroughly qualify prospects: Do they really want or need my product? Can they afford it? Can they make a buying commitment today?

4. Money matters

Money is a funny thing. People get very secretive about money, and very defensive. Get all money matters understood and written down in your notes before your presentation. You must avoid any mystery about money. Start out softly, "off the record," "in round numbers," then narrow the discussion down to specific dollar amounts.

5. Questions

Acting ignorant may come naturally to some people, but the new guerrilla may find it difficult. Asking lots of questions, even when you're certain of the answers, is essential. Ask what the prospect means. Don't try to be a mind reader. You must not presuppose any-thing. By eagerly answering prospect's questions, you may paint your-self into a corner with no escape. Ask counter-questions in response. Seek clarification and expansion. When prospects are positive and en-thusiastic, ask, "What makes you feel so good about this?" When prospects are pessimistic and negative, first agree: "I understand how you feel." Then ask, "Why do you feel that way? What exactly do you mean?"

Remember: name, rank, and serial number only. Anytime you think you ought to volunteer some information, pause to listen and ask a question instead. Guerrillas never help by trying to correct, ex-pand, or improve a prospect's statement. One of the worst things you could ever do in a selling situation is to fill in a prospect's sentence. You miss an opportunity to find out what the prospect is thinking and you'll probably appear rude.

6. Emotions

Guerrillas use emotions to sell to the prospect's unconscious wants and needs. Listen for all your prospect's articulated and undisclosed priorities. Prospects buy on emotions. At the deepest level, all deci-sions are emotional. We buy to improve our status, to feel good, to avoid pain, and to be well thought of in our community. Then we justify the decision with the facts. We tell ourselves and others that we bought because of the specific features and benefits found in the bro-chures and sales pamphlets.

About your own emotions, remember no one can enter your for-tress without your permission. You will be told "no" thousands of times. You're the one who must decide if people are going to hurt you personally.

7. Service

Guerrillas know the importance of always giving something extra in the Reward Step. Beyond that they are often asked for something more, like, "I need a quicker delivery." Rather than say, "Sure, I'll be glad to help you out," try something like: "That may be a bit difficult, but I know it's really important to you. I'll call you back after I've had a chance to check with our shipping department. Perhaps we can re-schedule a few things. We really do appreciate your business." This way, your customer will know that you've really gone out of your way, and that increases the perceived value of the effort, and really builds customer loyalty.

8. Battle plans

Guerrillas never do anything by accident. Planning is critical. Decide what you want, write up your battle plan, and you can bet on the result. Modern research has shown that the brain responds to a clear set of goals and mental visualization. Make your plans based on how many sales you're going to get each month. Plan on being "number one." Luck is preparation meeting opportunity. Guerrillas know how to get lucky: plan, prepare, and stay busy. Sales will come.

9. Fearlessness

Heroic bravery is not the absence of fear, but the ability to act in spite of it. We all share the experience of fear. It is part of our strategy for survival at some early phases of the Mind Map. Fear is the perception and anticipation of future danger, harm, or pain. Fear motivates us to avoid these potential problems.

Gallagher says everyone *always* has forty-nine problems. Fix one and something else will pop up and take its place! Make a list of your forty-nine, and when you can see them clearly, you will be well on the way to solving them and less likely to get caught in cycles of worry and fear.

One of the biggest fears is failure. If you are pinned down by enemy fire and you do nothing, you will get killed. Guerrillas know that *any* action, no matter how poorly planned or poorly executed, is safer than doing nothing. It's true that while not everyone always succeeds to their expectations, everyone always gets *some* result. The result that you get may not be the one you planned. In order to get a different result, you need only change the process and try again and, maybe, again. Guerrillas accept failure as part of the inevitable progress toward success. Keep at it. Take some action. Do it.

10. Attention

Many people get into sales because they know how to talk; they succeed to the degree that they learn how to listen. A guerrilla is hyper-aware, always on duty, listening for any threat or opportunity that might affect business. Guerrillas never complain or divulge negative information about their companies. Loose lips sink ships. The person sitting next to you on the airplane may become your next major account or a competitor. If your best client is in a slump, listen attentively, but don't commiserate by saying that your business is off, too.

Customers want to be able to rely on you. Remember you're a warrior, always on guard.

What makes the guerrilla different?

The guerrilla is the new soldier of fortune. As salespeople, they NaB & CaPTuRe new prospects the others miss, because they invest time, energy, and imagination in the process. Undermanned and under-equipped, they take on the corporate superpowers by turning *information* and *surprise* to their tactical advantage. And more often than not, they prevail over slick presentations and high-caliber marketing.

At the *Need* Stage, guerrillas gather massive amounts of intelligence about their prospects, their products, and their competitors before they ever call. They use the most modern discoveries in psychology to identify their prospects' personalities according to the *Mind Map*. They instantly pinpoint their prospects' priorities, criteria, and expectations.

Right up-front, in the *Budget* Stage, the guerrilla establishes the prospect's ability to pay by cost-justifying the price. The guerrilla sells on the basis of *value*, never on price alone. By questioning and carefully listening to the answers, the guerrilla determines the *progression* prospects will use to evaluate the product or service being offered. Understanding exactly how a prospect will decide to buy gives guerrillas an enormous advantage. They can target the strategic issues with surgical precision and ignore nonvital targets.

Guerrillas complete the *up-front close* at the *Commitment* Stage by aligning their proposal with issues to which the prospect is *already* committed. They verify the prospect's intent and ability to make a buying commitment *before* they start a sales presentation.

The guerrilla sales *Presentation* is customized to fit the communication style and personality of each individual prospect. This makes the guerrilla easy to understand and easy to do business with.

At the *Transaction* Stage, the customer, not the guerrilla, asks for the order. And when the prospect asks, the guerrilla *objects*. The prospect feels in total control, and no loose ends are left to booby-trap the sale later on.

Guerrillas *Reward* their customers for doing business with them. They find unique ways to say "thanks for the confidence you've shown in me and my company," a small gift, a special discount, or even a thoughtful handwritten note.

Guerrillas learn to *track* their customers doggedly, guaranteeing future sales through careful follow-up and never-let-you-down service. The sale is not the end of the battle for the guerrilla. In fact, there has never been a battle — the customer is your ally. The sale is often the beginning of a lifelong relationship.

Guerrillas are *fair* in all their dealings. They genuinely *care* about the people they serve and they let them know it. They do their *share*, by always giving their customers their money's worth and then some.

In the words of Albert Schweitzer:

> I don't know what your destiny will be,
> but one thing I do know:
> the only ones among you who will be really happy
> are those who have sought and found
> how to serve.

Your marching orders

Now you're armed and dangerous. You've trained and prepared a plan of attack. You've learned the prospects' strengths and weaknesses. You know how to NaB & CaPTuRe new customers and new markets. You've even got a map of how most people operate. Now there's only one thing left to do. Get out and fight for the business. We've got a job to do. Let's get on with it.

References and Recommended Reading, Listening, and Viewing for Guerrillas

Books

Albrecht, Karl, and Ron Zemke. *Service America!* Homewood, Ill.: Dow Jones-Irwin, 1985.

Alessandra, Tony, Phil Wexler, and Rick Barrera, *Non-Manipulative Selling.* 2nd ed. New York: Prentice Hall Press, 1987.

Arapakis, Maria. *Softpower!* New York: Warner Books, 1990.

Ash, Mary Kay. *Mary Kay on People Management.* New York: Warner Books, 1984.

Azar, Brian. *Be a Sales Doctor: Ease Your Prospect's Pain.* Rockaway, N.Y.: Sales Catalist, 1988.

Bandler, Richard, and John Grinder. *Reframing.* Boulder, Colo.: Real People Press, 1979.

Belasco, James A. *Teaching the Elephant to Dance.* New York: Crown, 1990.

Berne, Eric. *Games People Play.* New York: Ballantine, 1964.

Bettger, Frank. *How I Raised Myself from Failure to Success in Selling.* Engelwood Cliffs, N.J.: Prentice-Hall, 1975.

Black, Vern. *Love Me? Love Yourself.* San Francisco: Vern Black and Associates, 1983.

Blanchard, Kenneth, and Spencer Johnson. *The One Minute Manager.* New York: William Morrow and Co., 1982.

Blanchard, Kenneth, and Larry Wilson. *The One Minute Manager Meets the Monkey.* New York: William Morrow and Co., 1988.

Blechman, Bruce, and Jay Conrad Levinson. *Guerrilla Financing.* Boston: Houghton Mifflin, 1991.

Bliss, Edwin C. *Getting Things Done.* New York: Bantam, 1976.

————. *Doing It Now.* New York: Bantam, 1983.

Bury, Charles. *Telephone Techniques That Sell.* New York: Warner Books, 1980.

Cathcart, Jim. *Relationship Selling.* New York: Perigee Books, 1990.

Corsini, Raymond J. "Individual Education." *Journal of Individual Psychology* 33, no. 2a (1977).

Covey, Stephen R. *The Seven Habits of Highly Effective People.* New York: Simon and Schuster, 1989.

Danziger, Sanford, and R. K. Danziger. *You Are Your Own Best Counselor.* Honolulu: Self Mastery Systems International, 1984.

Davidow, William H., and Buro Uttal. *Total Customer Service: The Ultimate Weapon.* New York: Harper and Row, 1989.

[The editors.] "Are Your Prospects Worth Your Time and Energy?" *Personal Selling Power,* May–June 1989.

Enright, M. A., and N. Rosalind. "Is Your Customer An Extrovert, Introvert, Thinker, or Feeler?" *Personal Selling Power,* May–June 1989.

Fisher, R., and W. Ury. *Getting to Yes: Negotiating Agreement Without Giving In.* New York: Penguin Books, 1983.

Fuld, Leonard M. *Competitor Intelligence, How to Get It, How to Use It.* New York: John Wiley and Sons, 1985.

Gallagher, William K. "Meditation Simplified." *The Journal of Human Technology,* March 1984.

———. *Unlock the Full Potential of Your Mind.* Oakland, Calif.: Alto Press, 1986.

———. *The Neural Computer.* Oakland, Calif.: Alto Press, 1988.

Gerber, Michael E. *The E Myth.* Cambridge, Mass.: Ballinger Publishing, 1986.

Gilles, Jerry. *MoneyLove.* New York: Warner Books, 1978.

Girard, Joe, and Stanley H. Brown. *How to Sell Anything to Anybody.* New York: Warner Books, 1977.

Iacocca, Lee, with Sonny Kleinfield. *Lee Iacocca's Talking Straight.* New York: Bantam, 1988.

James, William. *The Principles of Psychology.* New York: Dover Publications, 1950 (original copyright, 1890).

Krashen, Stephen, and Richard Harshman. "Lateralization and the Critical Period." *Working Papers in Phonetics* (UCLA) 23 (June 1972).

Laborde, Gene Z. *Influencing With Integrity.* New York: Sintony, 1984.

LeBoeuf, Michael. *The Greatest Management Principle in the World.* New York: Berkley Books, 1985.

Levinson, Jay Conrad. *Guerrilla Marketing.* Boston: Houghton Mifflin, 1984.

———. *Guerrilla Marketing Attack.* Boston: Houghton Mifflin, 1987.

———. *Guerrilla Marketing Weapons.* New York: New American Library, Plume, 1990.

———. *The Ninety-Minute Hour.* New York: E. P. Dutton, 1990.

Levy, Bert. *Guerrilla Warfare.* Boulder, Colo.: Paladin Press, 1964.

Mackay, Harvey. *Swim With the Sharks Without Being Eaten Alive.* New York: Ivy Books, 1988.

———. *Beware the Naked Man Who Offers You His Shirt.* New York: Ivy Books, 1990.

Maltz, Maxwell. *Psychocybernetics*. New York: Pocket Books, 1960.

Maslow, Abraham. *Motivation and Personality*. New York: Harper and Row, 1954.

Naisbitt, John, and Patricia Aburdene. *Megatrends 2000*. New York: William Morrow and Co., 1990.

Ornstein, Robert E. *The Psychology of Consciousness*. New York: W. H. Freeman and Co., 1972.

Peters, Tom, and Robert Waterman. *In Search of Excellence*. New York: Warner Books, 1982.

Piaget, Jean. *Problems of Genetic Psychology*. Translated by A. Rosen. New York: Grossman Publishers, 1973.

Rackham, Neil. *Spin Selling*. New York: McGraw-Hill, 1988.

Restak, Richard M. *The Brain: The Last Frontier*. Garden City, N.Y.: Doubleday, 1979.

Riso, Don Richard. *Personality Types*. Boston: Houghton Mifflin, 1987.

Sagan, Carl. *Broca's Brain*. New York: Ballantine Books, 1973.

———. *The Dragons of Eden*. New York: Ballantine Books, 1977.

Schoonmaker, Alan N. *Negotiate to Win: Gaining the Psychological Edge*. Englewood Cliffs, N.J.: Prentice-Hall, 1988.

Schwartz, David. *The Magic of Thinking Big*. Englewood Cliffs, N.J.: Prentice-Hall, 1965.

Slutsky, Jeff. *Streetfighting: Low Cost Advertising Promotions for Your Business*. Englewood Cliffs, N.J.: Prentice-Hall, 1984.

Sperry, Roger W. "Perception in the Absence of Neocortical Commissures." *Perception and Its Disorders* (Association for Research in Nervous and Mental Diseases) 48 (1970).

Steinberg, Danny D., and Leon A. Jakobovits, eds. *Semantics: An Interdisciplinary Reader in Philosophy, Linguistics, and Psychology*. New York: Cambridge University Press, 1971.

Steiner, Rudolf. *Education As an Art*. Hudson, N.Y.: Anthrosophic Press, 1970.

Trisler, Hank. *No Bull Selling*. New York: Frederick Fell, 1983.

Toffler, Alvin. *Future Shock*. New York: Random House, 1970.

———. *Powershift*. New York: Bantam, 1990.

Van Lanker, Diana. "Heterogeneity in Language and Speech: Neurolinguistic Studies." *Working Papers in Phonetics* (UCLA) 29 (April 1975).

Walters, Dottie. *The Selling Power of a Woman*. North Hollywood, Calif.: Wilshire Book Co., 1986.

Walther, George. *Phone Power*. New York: G. P. Putnam's Sons, 1986.

Willingham, Ron. *Integrity Selling*. Garden City, N.Y.: Doubleday, 1987.

Ziglar, Zig. *Secrets of Closing the Sale*. New York: Berkley Books, 1984.

Zinsser, William. *On Writing Well*. New York: Harper and Row, 1988.

Zunin, Leonard. *Contact: The First Four Minutes*. New York: Ballantine Books, 1988.

Audio tapes[1]

Arapakis, Maria. "How to Speak Up, Set Limits, and Say No." Boulder, Colo.: CareerTrack Publications, 1987.

Battles, Brian. "How to Listen Powerfully." Boulder, Colo.: CareerTrack Publications, 1988.

Bliss, Edwin. "Getting Things Done." Boulder, Colo.: CareerTrack Publications, 1985.

Brinkman, Rick, and Rick Kirschner. "How to Deal With Difficult People." Boulder, Colo.: CareerTrack Publications, 1987.

Canfield, Jack. "Self-Esteem and Peak Performance." Boulder, Colo.: CareerTrack Publications, 1987.

Cathcart, Jim, and Anthony Alessandra. "Relationship Strategies." Chicago: Nightingale-Conant, 1985.

Gallagher, Bill. "The Mind Map." San Diego, Calif.: Guerrilla Associates, 1989.

Gallagher, Bill, and Orvel Ray Wilson. "Guerrilla Selling." San Diego, Calif.: Guerrilla Associates, 1990.

Garfield, Charles. "Peak Performers." Chicago: Nightingale-Conant, 1986.

Merrill, Douglas. "The New Time Management." Chicago: Nightingale-Conant, 1983.

Moidel, Steve. "Memory Power." Boulder, Colo.: CareerTrack Publications, 1989.

Peters, Tom. "The New Masters of Excellence." Chicago: Nightingale-Conant, 1988.

———. "Thriving on Chaos." Chicago: Nightingale-Conant, 1988.

Robbins, Anthony. "Unlimited Power." Chicago: Nightingale-Conant, 1989.

Smith, Debra. "Telephone Skills." Boulder, Colo.: CareerTrack Publications, 1987.

Sommer, Bobbe. "How to Set and Achieve Goals." Boulder, Colo.: CareerTrack Publications, 1987.

Tracy, Brian. "The Psychology of Achievement." Chicago: Nightingale-Conant, 1988.

Wilson, Orvel Ray. "Sell Like the Pros." Boulder, Colo.: CareerTrack Publications, 1990.

[1]To order audio and video materials, call the Guerrilla Group at 1-800-247-9145, CareerTrack Publications at 1-800-334-1018, or Nightingale-Conant Corp. at 1-800-323-5552.

Video training materials

Gallagher, William K. "The Mind Map." San Diego, Calif.: Guerrilla Associates, 1990.

Sanborn, Mark. "Team Building," Vols. 1 and 2. Boulder, Colo.: CareerTrack Publications, 1989.

Smith, Debra. "Professional Telephone Skills." Boulder, Colo.: CareerTrack Publications, 1989.

Index

Notes

Notes

Notes

CONTINUE BEING A GUERRILLA

Call us toll-free 1-800-247-9145 for a free brochure on:

- **Guerrilla Selling**
- **Guerrilla Marketing**
- **Guerrilla Management**

Customized guerrilla sales training programs are available.

We also offer books, audiotapes, videotapes, newsletters, seminars, lectures, workshops and other professional services.

Sales and marketing consulting is available to groups and individuals.

The Guerrilla Group
P.O. Box 2050
741 N. Circle
Diamond Springs, CA 95619
1-800-800-8086